SEVEN
ENGLISH CITIES

W. D. HOWELLS

1st WORLD
LIBRARY
Literary Society

Seven English Cities

W. D. Howells

© 1st World Library, 2007
PO Box 2211
Fairfield, IA 52556
www.1stworldlibrary.com
First Edition

LCCN: 2007930819

Softcover ISBN: 978-1-4218-4862-4
Hardcover ISBN: 978-1-4218-4765-8
eBook ISBN: 978-1-4218-4959-1

Purchase *"Seven English Cities"*
as a traditional bound book at:
www.1stWorldLibrary.com/purchase.asp?ISBN=978-1-4218-4862-4

1st World Library is a literary, educational organization dedicated to:

- Creating a free internet library of downloadable ebooks

- Hosting writing competitions and offering book publishing scholarships.

Interested in more 1st World Library books? contact:
literacy@1stworldlibrary.com
Check us out at: www.1stworldlibrary.com

1ˢᵗ World Library Literary Society

Giving Back to the World

"If you want to work on the core problem, it's early school literacy."

- James Barksdale, former CEO of Netscape

"No skill is more crucial to the future of a child, or to a democratic and prosperous society, than literacy."

- Los Angeles Times

"Literacy... means far more than learning how to read and write... The aim is to transmit... knowledge and promote social participation."

- UNESCO

"Literacy is not a luxury, it is a right and a responsibility. If our world is to meet the challenges of the twenty-first century we must harness the energy and creativity of all our citizens."

- President Bill Clinton

"Parents should be encouraged to read to their children, and teachers should be equipped with all available techniques for teaching literacy, so the varying needs and capacities of individual kids can be taken into account."

- Hugh Mackay

CONTENTS

A MODEST LIKING FOR LIVERPOOL

Why should the proud stomach of American travel, much tossed in the transatlantic voyage, so instantly have itself carried from Liverpool to any point where trains will convey it? Liverpool is most worthy to be seen and known, and no one who looks up from the bacon and eggs of his first hotel breakfast after landing, and finds himself confronted by the coal-smoked Greek architecture of St. George's Hall, can deny that it is of a singularly noble presence. The city has moments of failing in the promise of this classic edifice, but every now and then it reverts to it, and reminds the traveller that he is in a great modern metropolis of commerce by many other noble edifices.

I

Liverpool does not remind him of this so much as the good
and true Baedeker professes, in the dockside run on the
overhead railway (as the place unambitiously calls its
elevated road); but then, as I noted in my account of
Southampton, docks have a fancy of taking themselves in,
and eluding the tourist eye, and even when they "flank the
Mersey for a distance of 6-7 M." they do not respond to
American curiosity so frankly as could be wished. They are
like other English things in that, however, and it must be said
for them that when apparent they are sometimes unim-
pressive. From my own note-book, indeed, I find that I
pretended to think them "wonderful and almost endless," and
so I dare say they are. But they formed only a very
perfunctory interest of our day at Liverpool, where we had
come to meet, not to take, a steamer.

Our run from London, in the heart of June, was very quick
and pleasant, through a neat country and many tidy towns. In
the meadows the elms seemed to droop like our own rather
than to hold themselves oakenly upright like the English; the
cattle stood about in the yellow buttercups, knee-deep, white
American daisies, and red clover, and among the sheep we
had our choice of shorn and unshorn; they were equally
abundant. Some of the blossomy May was left yet on the
hawthorns, and over all the sky hovered, with pale-white
clouds in pale-blue spaces of air like an inverted lake of
bonnyclabber. We stopped the night at Chester, and the next
evening, in the full daylight of 7.40, we pushed on to
Liverpool, over lovely levels, with a ground swell like that of
Kansas plains, under a sunset drying its tears and at last
radiantly smiling.

W. D. Howells

II

The hotel in Liverpool swarmed and buzzed with busy and murmurous American arrivals. One could hardly get at the office window, on account of them, to plead for a room. A dense group of our countrywomen were buying picture-postals of the rather suave office-ladies, and helplessly fawning on them in the inept confidences of American women with all persons in official or servile attendance. "Let me stay here," one of them entreated, "because there's such a draught at the other window. May I?" She was a gentle child of forty-five or fifty; and I do not know whether she was allowed to stay in the sheltered nook or not, tender creature. As she was in every one else's way there, possibly she was harshly driven into the flaw at the other window.

The place was a little America which swelled into a larger with the arrivals of the successive steamers, though the soft swift English trains bore our co-nationals away as rapidly as they could. Many familiar accents remained till the morning, and the breakfast-room was full of a nasal resonance which would have made one at home anywhere in our East or West. I, who was then vainly trying to be English, escaped to the congenial top of the farthest bound tram, and flew, at the rate of four miles an hour, to the uttermost suburbs of Liverpool, whither no rumor of my native speech could penetrate. It was some balm to my wounded pride of country to note how pale and small the average type of the local people was. The poorer classes swarmed along a great part of the tram-line in side streets of a hard, stony look, and what characterized itself to me as a sort of iron squalor seemed to prevail. You cannot anywhere have great prosperity without great adversity, just as you cannot have day without night, and the more Liverpool evidently flourished the more it plainly languished. I found no pleasure in the paradox, and I was not overjoyed by the inevitable ugliness of the brick villas of the suburbs into which these obdurate streets decayed. But then, after divers tram changes, came the consolation of beautiful riverside beaches, thronged with people who looked gay at that distance, and beyond the Mersey rose the Welsh hills, blue, blue.

W. D. Howells

III

At the end of the tram-line, where we necessarily dismounted, we rejected a thatched cottage, offering us tea, because we thought it too thatched and too cottage to be quite true (though I do not now say that there were vermin in the straw roof), and accepted the hospitality of a pastry-cook's shop. We felt the more at home with the kind woman who kept it because she had a brother at Chicago in the employ of the Pinkerton Detective Agency, and had once been in Stratford-on-Avon; this doubly satisfied us as cultivated Americans. She had a Welsh name, and she testified to a great prevalence of Welsh and Irish in the population of Liverpool; besides, she sent us to a church of the Crusaders at Little Crosby, and it was no fault of hers that we did not find it. We found one of the many old crosses for which Little Crosby is named, and this was quite as much as we merited. It stood at the intersection of the streets in what seemed the fragment of a village, not yet lost in the vast maw of the city, and it calmed all the simple neighborhood, so that we sat down at its foot and rested a long, long minute till the tram came by and took us back into the loud, hard heart of Liverpool.

I do not mean to blame it, for it was no louder or harder than the hearts of other big towns, and it had some alleviation from the many young couples who were out together half-holidaying in the unusually pleasant Saturday weather. I wish their complexions had been better, but you cannot have South-of-England color if you live as far north as Liverpool, and all the world knows what the American color is. The young couples abounded in the Gallery of Fine Arts, where they frankly looked at one another instead of the pictures. The pictures might have been better, but then they might have been worse (there being examples of Filippo Lippi,

Memmi, Holbein, and, above all, the *Dante's Dream* of Rossetti); and in any case those couples could come and see them when they were old men and women; but now they had one another in a moment of half-holiday which could not last forever.

In the evening there were not so many lovers at the religious meetings before the classic edifice opposite the hotel, where the devotions were transacted with the help of a brass-band; but there were many youths smoking short pipes, and flitting from one preacher to another, in the half-dozen groups. Some preachers were nonconformist, but there was one perspiring Anglican priest who labored earnestly with his hearers, and who had more of his aspirates in the right place. Many of his hearers were in the rags which seem a favorite wear in Liverpool, and I hope his words did their poor hearts good.

Slightly apart from the several congregations, I found myself with a fellow-foreigner of seafaring complexion who addressed me in an accent so unlike my own American that I ventured to answer him in Italian. He was indeed a Genoese, who had spent much time in Buenos Ayres and was presently thinking of New York; and we had some friendly discourse together concerning the English. His ideas of them were often so parallel with my own that I hardly know how to say he thought them an improvident people. I owned that they spent much more on state, or station, than the Americans; but we neither had any censure for them other-wise. He was of that philosophic mind which one is rather apt to encounter in the Latin races, and I could well wish for his further acquaintance. His talk rapt me to far other and earlier scenes, and I seemed to be conversing with him under a Venetian heaven, among objects of art more convincing than the equestrian statue of the late Queen, who had no special motive I could think of for being shown to her rightly

W. D. Howells

loving subjects on horseback. We parted with the expressed hope of seeing each other again, and if this should meet his eye and he can recall the pale young man, with the dark full beard, who chatted with him between the pillars of the Piazzetta, forty years before our actual encounter I would be glad of his address.

IV

How strange are the uses of travel! There was a time when the mention of Liverpool would have conjured up for me nothing but the thought of Hawthorne, who spent divers dull consular years there, and has left a record of them which I had read, with the wish that it were cheerfuler. Yet, now, here on the ground his feet might have trod, and in the very smoke he breathed, I did not once think of him. I thought as little of that poor Felicia Hemans, whose poetry filled my school-reading years with the roar of the wintry sea breaking from the waveless Plymouth Bay on the stern and rock-bound coast where the Pilgrim Fathers landed on a bowlder measuring eight by ten feet, now fenced in against the predatory hammers and chisels of reverent visitors. I knew that Gladstone was born at Liverpool, but not Mrs. Oliphant, and the only literary shade I could summon from a past vague enough to my ignorance was William Roscoe, whose *Life of Leo X.*, in the Bohn Library, had been too much for my young zeal when my zeal was still young. My other memories of Liverpool have been acquired since my visit, and I now recur fondly to the picturesque times when King John founded a castle there, to the prouder times when Sir Francis Bacon represented it in Parliament; or again to the brave days when it resisted Prince Rupert for three weeks, and the inglorious epoch when the new city (it was then only some four or five hundred years old) began to flourish on the trade in slaves with the colonies of the Spanish Main, and on the conjoint and congenial traffic in rum, sugar, and tobacco.

It will be suspected from these reminiscences that I have been studying a page of fine print in Baedeker, and I will not deceive the reader. It is true; but it is also true that I had some wonder, altogether my own, that so great a city should make so small an appeal to the imagination. In this it outdoes

W. D. Howells

almost any metropolis of our own. Even in journalism, an intensely modern product, it does not excel; Manchester has its able and well- written *Guardian*, but what has Liverpool? Glasgow has its Glasgow School of Painting, but again what has Liverpool? It is said that not above a million of its people live in it; all the rest, who can, escape to Chester, where they perhaps vainly hope to escape the Americans. There, intrenched in charming villas behind myrtle hedges, they measurably do so; but Americans are very penetrating, and I would not be sure that the thickest and highest hedge was invulnerable to them. As it is, they probably constitute the best society of Liverpool, which the natives have abandoned to them, though they do not constitute it permanently, but consecutively. Every Cunarder, every White Star, pours out upon a city abandoned by its own good society a flood of cultivated Americans, who eddy into its hotels, and then rush out of them by every train within twenty-four hours, and often within twenty-five minutes. They understand that there are no objects of interest in Liverpool; and they are not met at the Customs with invitations to breakfast, luncheon, and dinner from the people of rank and fashion with whom they have come to associate. These have their stately seats in the lovely neighboring country, but they are not at the landing-stage, and even the uncultivated American cannot stay for the vast bourgeoisie of which Liverpool, like the cities of his own land, is composed. Our own cities have a social consciousness, and are each sensible of being a centre, with a metropolitan destiny; but the strange thing about Liverpool and the like English towns is that they are without any social consciousness. Their meek millions are socially unborn; they can come into the world only in London, and in their prenatal obscurity they remain folded in a dreamless silence, while all the commercial and industrial energies rage round them in a gigantic maturity.

V

The time was when Liverpool was practically the sole port of entry for our human cargoes, indentured apprentices of the beautiful, the historical. With the almost immediate transference of the original transatlantic steamship interests from Bristol, Liverpool became the only place where you could arrive. American lines, long erased from the seas, and the Inman line, the Cunard line, the White Star line, and the rest, would land you nowhere else. Then heretical steamers began to land you at Glasgow; worse schismatics carried you to Southampton; there were heterodox craft that touched at Plymouth, and now great swelling agnostics bring you to London itself. Still, Liverpool remains the greatest port of entry for our probationers, who are bound out to the hotels and railroad companies of all Europe till they have morally paid back their fare. The superstition that if you go in a Cunarder you can sleep on both ears is no longer so exclusive as it once was; yet the Cunarder continues an ark of safety for the timid and despairing, and the cooking is so much better than it used to be that if in contravention of the old Cunard rule against a passenger's being carried over-board you do go down, you may be reasonably sure of having eaten something that the wallowing sea-monsters will like in you.

I have tried to give some notion of the fond behavior of the arriving Americans in the hotels; no art can give the impression of their exceeding multitude. Expresses, panting with as much impatience as the disciplined English expresses ever suffer themselves to show, await them in the stations, which are effectively parts of the great hotels, and whir away to London with them as soon as they can drive up from the steamer; but many remain to rest, to get the sea out of their heads and legs, and to prepare their spirits for adjustment to

W. D. Howells

the novel conditions. These the successive trains carry into the heart of the land everywhere, these and their baggage, to which they continue attached by their very heart-strings, invisibly stretching from their first-class corridor compartments to the different luggage- vans. I must say they have very tenderly, very perfectly imagined us, all those hotel people and railroad folk, and fold us, anxious and bewildered exiles, in a reassuring and consoling embrace which leaves all their hands—they are Briarean—free for the acceptance of our wide, wild tips. You may trust yourself implicitly to their care, but if you are going to Oxford do not trust the head porter who tells you to take the London and Northwestern, for then you will have to change four times on the way and at every junction personally see that your baggage is unladen and started anew to its destination.

* * * * *

SOME MERITS OF MANCHESTER

I will suppose the reader not to be going to Oxford, but, in compliance with the scheme of this paper, to Manchester, where there is perhaps no other reason for his going. He will there, for one thing, find the supreme type of the railroad hotel which in England so promptly shelters and so kindly soothes the fluttered exile. At Manchester, even more than at Liverpool, we are imagined in the immense railroad station hotel, which is indeed perhaps superorganized and over-convenienced after an American ideal: one does not, for instance, desire a striking, or even a ticking, clock in the transom above one's bedroom door; but the like type of hotel is to be found at every great railroad centre or terminal in England, and it is never to be found quite bad, though of course it is sometimes better and sometimes worse. It is hard to know if it is more hotel or more station; perhaps it is a mixture of each which defies analysis; but in its well-studied composition you pass, as it were, from your car to your room, as from one chamber to another. This is putting the fact poetically; but, prosaically, the intervening steps are few at the most; and when you have entered your room your train has ceased to be. The simple miracle would be impossible in America, where our trains, when not shrieking at the tops of their whistles, are backing and filling with a wild clangor of their bells, and making a bedlam of their stations; but in England they

W. D. Howells

"Come like shadows, so depart,"

and make no sound within the vast caravansary where the enchanted traveller has changed from them into a world of dreams.

I

These hotels are, next to the cathedrals, perhaps the greatest wonder of England, and in Manchester the railway hotel is in some ways more wonderful than the cathedral, which is not so much planned on our native methods. Yet this has the merit, if it is a merit, of antedating our Discovery by nearly a century, and pre- historically it is indefinitely older. My sole recorded impression of it is that I found it smelling strongly of coal-gas, such as comes up the register when your furnace is mismanaged; but that is not strange in such a manu-facturing centre; and it would be paltering with the truth not to own a general sense of the beauty and grandeur in it which no English cathedral is without. The morning was fitly dim and chill, and one could move about in the vague all the more comfortably for the absence of that appeal of thronging monuments which harasses and bewilders the visitor in other cathedrals; one could really give one's self up to serious emotion, and not be sordidly and rapaciously concerned with objects of interest. Manchester has been an episcopal see only some fifty years; before that the cathedral was simply T' Owd Church, and in this character it is still venerable, and is none the less so because of the statue of Oliver Cromwell which holds the chief place in the open square before it. Call it an incongruity, if you will, but that enemy of episcopacy is at least not accused of stabling his horses in The Old Church at Manchester, or despoiling it of its sacred images and stained glass, and he merits a monument there if anywhere.

With the constantly passing trams which traverse the square, he is undoubtedly more significant of modern Manchester than the episcopacy is, and perhaps of that older Manchester which held for him against the king, and that yet older Manchester of John Bradford, the first martyr of the Refor-mation to suffer death at the stake in Smithfield. Of the still

W. D. Howells

yet older, far older Manchester, which trafficked with the Greeks of Marseilles, and later passed under the yoke of Agricola and was a Roman military station, and got the name of Maen-ceaster from the Saxons, and was duly bedevilled by the Danes and mishandled by the Normans, there may be traces in the temperament of the modern town which would escape even the scrutiny of the hurried American. Such a compatriot was indeed much more bent upon getting a pair of cotton socks, like those his own continent wears almost universally in summer, but a series of exhaustive visits to all the leading haberdashers in Manchester developed the strange fact that there, in the world-heart of the cotton-spinning industry, there was no such thing to be found. In Manchester there are only woollen socks, heavier or lighter, to be bought, and the shopmen smile pityingly if you say, in your strange madness, that woollen socks are not for summer wear. Possibly, however, it was not summer in Manchester, and we were misled by the almanac. Possibly we had been spoiled by three weeks of warm, sunny rain on the Welsh coast, and imagined a vain thing in supposing that the end of August was not the beginning of November.

II

I thought Manchester, however, as it shows itself in its public edifices, a most dignified town, with as great beauty as could be expected of a place which has always had so much to do besides looking after its figure and complexion. The very charming series or system of parks, public gardens, and playgrounds, unusual in their number and variety, had a sympathetic allure in the gray, cool light, even to the spectator passing in a hurried hansom. They have not the unity of the Boston or Chicago parkways, and I will own that I had not come to Manchester for them. What interested me more were the miles and miles of comfortable- looking little brick houses in which, for all I knew, the mill- labor dwelt. Very possibly it did not; the mills themselves are now nearly all, or mostly, outside of Manchester, and perhaps for this reason I did not find the slums, when shown them, very slummy, and I saw no such dreadful shapes of rags and dirt as in Liverpool. We passed through a quarter of large, old-fashioned mansions, as charming as they were unimagined of Manchester; but these could not have been the dwellings of the mill-hands, any more than of the mill-owners. The mill-owners, at least, live in suburban palaces and villas, which I fancy by this time are not

—"pricking a cockney ear,"

as in the time of Tennyson's "Maud."

What wild and whirling insolences, however, the people who have greatly made the greatness of England have in all times suffered from their poets and novelists, with few exceptions! One need not be a very blind devotee of commercialism or industrialism to resent the affronts put upon them, when one comes to the scenes of such mighty achievement as

W. D. Howells

Liverpool, and Manchester, and Sheffield; but how mildly they seem to have taken it all—with what a meek subordination and sufferance! One asks one's self whether the society of such places can be much inferior to that of Pittsburg, or Chicago, or St. Louis, which, even from the literary attics of New York, we should not exactly allow ourselves to spit upon. Practically, I know nothing about society in Manchester, or rather, out of it; and I can only say of the general type, of richer or poorer, as I saw it in the streets, that it was uncommonly good. Not so many women as men were abroad in such weather as we had, and I cannot be sure that the sex shows there that superiority physically which it has long held morally with us. One learns in the north not to look for the beautiful color of the south and west; but in Manchester the average faces were intelligent and the figures good.

III

With such a journal as the Manchester *Guardian* still keeping its high rank among English newspapers, there cannot be question of the journalistic sort of thinking in the place. Of the sort that comes to its effect in literature, such as, say, Mrs. Gaskell's novels, there may also still be as much as ever; and I will not hazard my safe ignorance in a perilous conjecture. I can only say that of the Unitarianism which eventuated in that literature, I heard it had largely turned to episcopacy, as Unitarianism has in our own Boston. I must not forget that one of our religions, now a dying faith, was invented in Manchester by Ann Lee, who brought, through the usual persecutions, Shakerism to such spiritual importance as it has now lost in these States. Only those who have known the Shakers, with their good lives and gentle ways, can regret with me the decline of the celibate communism which their foundress imagined in her marital relations with the Lancashire blacksmith she left behind her.

I am reminded (or perhaps instructed) by Mr. Hope Moncrieff in Black's excellent *Guide to Manchester* that before Mrs. Gaskell's celebrity the fitful fame of De Quincey shed a backward gleam upon his native place, which can still show the house where he was probably born and the grammar-school he certainly ran away from. In my forgetfulness, or my ignorance, that Manchester was the mother of this tricksy master-spirit of English prose, who was an idol of my youth, I failed to visit either house. The renown of Cobden and of Bright is precious to a larger world than mine; and the name of the stalwart Quaker friend of man is dear to every American who remembers the heroic part he played in our behalf during our war for the Union. It is one of the amusing anomalies of the British constitution, that the great city from whose political fame these names are inseparable should have had no representation in Parliament from Cromwell's time to Victoria's. Fancy Akron, Ohio, or Grand Rapids, Michigan, without a member of Congress!

The "Manchester school" of political economy has long since passed into reproach if not obloquy with people for whom a byword is a potent weapon, and perhaps the easiest they can handle, and I am not myself so extreme a *laissez-faireist* as to have thought of that school with pathos in the city of its origin; but I dare say it was a good thing in its time. We are only now slowly learning how to apply the opposite social principles in behalf of the Man rather than the Master, and we have not yet surmounted all the difficulties or dangers of the experiment. It is droll how, in a tolerably well-meaning world like this, any sort of contempt becomes inclusive, and a whole population suffers for the vice, or it may be the virtue, of a very small majority, or a very powerful minority. Probably the most liberal and intelligent populations of Great Britain are those of Manchester and Birmingham, names which have stood for a hard and sordid industrialism, unrelieved by noble sympathies and impulses. It is quite possible that a less generous spirit than mine would have censured the "Manchester school" for the weather of the place, and found in its cold gray light the effect of the Gradgrind philosophy which once wrapt a world of fiction in gloom.

IV

I can only be sure that the light, what little there was of it, was very cold and gray, but it quite sufficed to show the huge lowries, as the wagons are called, passing through the streets with the cotton fabrics of the place in certain stages of manufacture: perhaps the raw, perhaps the finished material. In Manchester itself one sees not much else of "the cotton-spinning chorus" which has sent its name so far. The cotton is now spun in ten or twenty towns in the nearer or farther neighborhood of the great city, as every one but myself and some ninety millions of other Americans well know. I had seen something of cotton-mills in our Lowell, and I was eager, if not willing, to contrast them with the mills of Manchester; but such of these as still remained there were, for my luckless moment, inoperative. Personal influences brought me within one or two days of their starting up; one almost started up during my brief stay; but a great mill, employing perhaps a thousand hands, cannot start up for the sake of the impression desired by the aesthetic visitor, and I had to come away without mine.

I had to come away without that personal acquaintance with the great Manchester ship-canal which I almost equally desired. Coming or going, I asked about it, and was told, looking for it from the car window, there, *there* it was! but beyond a glimpse of something very long and very straight marking the landscape with lines no more convincing than those which science was once decided, and then undecided, to call canals on the planet Mars, I had no sight of it. I do not say this was not my fault; and I will not pretend that the canal, like the mills of Manchester, was not running. I dare say I was not in the right hands, but this was not for want of trying to get into them. In the local delusion that it was then summer, those whose kindness might have befriended the ignorance of the stranger were "away on their holidays": that was exactly the phrase.

When, by a smiling chance, I fell into the right hands and was borne to the Cotton Exchange I did not fail of a due sense of the important scene, I hope. The building itself, like the other public buildings of Manchester, is most dignified, and the great hall of the exchange is very noble. I would not, if I could, have repressed a thrill of pride in seeing our national colors and emblems equalled with those of Great Britain at one end of the room, but these were the only things American in the impression left. We made our way through the momently thickening groups on the floor, and in the guidance of a member of the exchange found a favorable point of observation in the gallery. From this the vast space below showed first a moving surface of hats, with few silk toppers among them, but a multitude of panamas and other straws. The marketing was not carried on with anything like the wild, rangy movement of our Stock Exchange, and the floor sent up no such hell-roaring (there is no other phrase for it) tumult as rises from the mad but not malign demons of that most dramatic representation of perdition. The merchants, alike staid, whether old or young, congregated in groups which, dealing in a common type of goods, kept the same places till, toward three o'clock, they were lost in the mass which covered the floor. Even then there was no uproar, no rush or push, no sharp cries or frenzied shouting; but from the crowd, which was largely made up of elderly men, there rose a sort of surd, rich hum, deepening ever, and never breaking into a shriek of torment or derision. It was not histrionic, and yet for its commercial importance it was one of the most moving spectacles which could offer itself to the eye in the whole world.

I cannot pretend to have profited by my visit to that immensely valuable deposit of books, bought from the

Spencer family at Althorp, and dedicated as the Rylands library to the memory of a citizen of Manchester. Books in a library, except you have time and free access to them, are as baffling as so many bottles in a wine-cellar, which are not opened for you, and which if they were would equally go to your head without final advantage. I find, therefore, that my sole note upon the Rylands Library is the very honest one that it smelt, like the cathedral, of coal-gas. The absence of this gas was the least merit of the beautiful old Chetham College, with its library dating from the seventeenth century, and claiming to have been the first free library in England, and doubtless the world. In the cloistered picturesqueness of the place, its mediaeval memorials, and its ancient peace, I found myself again in those dear Middle Ages which are nowhere quite wanting in England, and against which I rubbed off all smirch of the modernity I had come to Manchester for.

* * * * *

W. D. Howells

IN SMOKIEST SHEFFIELD

If I had waited a little till I had got into the beautiful Derbyshire country which lies, or rather rolls, between Manchester and Sheffield, I could as easily have got rid of my epoch in the smiling agricultural landscape. I do not know just the measure of the Black Country in England, or where Sheffield begins to be perhaps the blackest spot in it; but I am sure that nothing not surgically clean could be whiter than the roads that, almost as soon as we were free of Manchester, began to climb the green, thickly wooded hills, and dip into the grassy and leafy valleys. In the very heart of the loveliness we found Sheffield most nobly posed against a lurid sunset, and clouding the sky, which can never be certain of being blue, with the smoke of a thousand towering chimneys. From whatever point you have it, the sight is most prodigious, but no doubt the subjective sense of the great ducal mansions and estates which neighbor the mirky metropolis of steel and iron has its part in heightening the dramatic effect.

I

The English, with their love of brevity and simplicity, call these proud seats the Dukeries, but our affair was not with them, and I shall not be able to follow the footmen or butlers or housekeepers who would so obligingly show them to the reader in my company. I had a fine consciousness of passing some of them on my way into the town, and when there of being, however, incongruously, in the midst of them. Worksop, more properly than Sheffield, is the plebeian heart of these aristocratic homes, or sojourns, which no better advised traveller, or less hurried, will fail to see. But I was in Sheffield to see the capital of the Black Country in its most characteristic aspects, and I thought it felicitously in keeping, after I had dined (less well than I could have wished, at the railway hotel which scarcely kept the promise made for it by other like hotels) that I should be tempted beyond my strength to go and see that colored opera which we had lately sent, after its signal success with us, to an even greater prosperity in England. *In Dahomey* is a musical drama not pitched in the highest key, but it is a genuine product of our national life, and to witness its performance by the colored brethren who invented it, and were giving it with great applause in an atmosphere quite undarkened by our racial prejudices, was an experience which I would not have missed for many Dukeries. The kindly house was not so suffocatingly full that it could not find breath for cheers and laughter; but I proudly felt that no one there could delight so intelligently as the sole American, in the familiar Bowery figures, the blue policemen, the varying darky types, which peopled a scene largely laid in Africa. The local New York suggestions were often from Mr. Edward Harrigan, and all the more genuine for that, but there was a final cake-walk which owed its inspiration wholly to the genius of a race destined to greater triumphs in music and art, and perhaps to

W. D. Howells

a kindlier civilization than our ideals have evolved in yet. It was pleasant to look upon those different shades of color, from dead black to creamy blond, in their novel relief against an air of ungrudging, of even respectful, appreciation, and I dare say the poor things liked it for themselves as much as I liked it for them. At a fine moment of the affair I was aware of a figure in evening dress, standing near me, and regarding the stage with critical severity: a young man, but shrewd and well in hand, who, as the unmistakable manager, was, I hope, finally as well satisfied as the other spectators.

II

I myself came away entirely satisfied, indeed, but for the lasting pang I inflicted upon myself by denying a penny to the ragged wretch who superfluously opened the valves of my hansom for me. My explanation to my soul was that I had no penny in my pocket, and that it would have been folly little short of crime to give so needy a wretch sixpence. But would it? Would it have corrupted him, since pauperize him further it could not? I advise the reader who finds himself in the like case to give the sixpence, and if he cares for the peace of my conscience, to make it a shilling; or, come! a half-crown, if he wishes to be truly handsome. It is astonishing how these regrets persist; but perhaps in this instance I owe the permanence of my pang to those frequent appeals to one's pity which repeated themselves in Sheffield. As I had noted at Liverpool I now noted at Sheffield that you cannot have great prosperity without having adversity, just as you cannot have heat without cold or day without dark. The one substantiates and verifies the other; and I perceived that wherever business throve it seemed to be at the cost of somebody; though even when business pines it is apparently no better. The thing ought to be looked into.

At the moment of my visit to Sheffield, it happened that many works were running half-time or no time, and many people were out of work. At one place there was a little oblong building between branching streets, round which sat a miserable company of Murchers, as I heard them called, on long benches under the overhanging roof, who were too obviously, who were almost offensively, out of work. Some were old and some young, some dull and some fierce, some savage and some imbecile in their looks, and they were all stained and greasy and dirty, and looked their apathy or their grim despair. Even the men who were coming to or from

W. D. Howells

their work at dinner-time looked stunted and lean and pale, with no color of that south of England bloom with which they might have favored a stranger. Slatternly girls and women abounded, and little babies carried about by a little larger babies, and of course kissed on their successive layers of dirt. There were also many small boys who, I hope, were not so wicked as they were ragged. At noon-time they hung much about the windows of cookshops which one would think their sharp hunger would have pierced to the steaming and smoking dishes within. The very morning after I had denied that man a penny at the theatre door, and was still smarting to think I had not given him sixpence, I saw a boy of ten, in the cut-down tatters of a man, gloating upon a meat-pie which a cook had cruelly set behind the pane in front of him. I took out the sixpence which I ought to have given that poor man, and made it a shilling, and put it into the boy's wonderfully dirty palm, and bade him go in and get the pie. He looked at me, and he looked at the shilling, and then I suppose he did as he was bid. But I ought to say, in justice to myself, that I never did anything of the kind again as long as I remained in Sheffield. I felt that I owed a duty to the place and must not go about corrupting the populace for my selfish pleasure.

III

Between our hotel and the main part of the town there yawned a black valley, rather nobly bridged, or viaducted, and beyond it in every direction the chimneys of the many works thickened in the perspectives. It was really like a dead forest, or like thick-set masts of shipping in a thronged port; or the vents of tellurian fires, which send up their flames by night and their smoke by day. It was splendid, it was magnificent, it was insurpassably picturesque. People must have painted it often, but if some bravest artist-soul would come, reverently, not patronizingly, and portray the sight in its naked ugliness, he would create one of the most beautiful masterpieces in the world. On our first morning the sun, when it climbed to the upper heavens, found a little hole in the dun pall, and shone down through it, and tried to pierce through the more immediate cloud above the works; but it could not, and it ended by shutting the hole under it, and disappearing.

Beyond the foul avenues thridding the region of the works, and smelling of the decay of market-houses, were fine streets of shops and churches, and I dare say comely dwellings, with tram- cars ascending and descending their hilly slopes. The stores I find noted as splendid, and in my pocket-book I say that outside of the market-house, before you got to those streets, there are doves and guinea-pigs as well as a raven for sale in cages; and the usual horrible English display of flesh meats. The trams were one story, like our trolleys, without roof-seats, and there were plenty of them; but nothing could keep me, I suppose, till I had seen one of the works. Each of these stands in a vast yard, or close, by itself, with many buildings, and they are of all sorts; but I chose what I thought the most typical, and overcame the reluctance of the manager to let me see it. He said I had no idea what tricks were played

W. D. Howells

by other makers to find out any new processes and steal them; but this was after I had pleaded my innocent trade of novelist, and assured him of my congenital incapability of understanding, much less conveying from the premises, the image of the simplest and oldest process. Then he gave me for guide an intelligent man who was a penknife-maker by trade, but was presently out of work, and glad to earn my fee.

My guide proved a most decent, patient, and kindly person, and I hope it is no betrayal of confidence to say that he told me the men in these multitudinous shops work by the piece. The grinders furnish their grindstones and all their tools for making the knives; there is no dry grinding, such as used to fill the lungs of the grinders with deadly particles of steel and stone, and bring them to an early death; but sometimes a stone, which ordinarily lasts six months, will burst and drive the grinder through the roof. The blade-makers do their own forging and hammering, and it is from first to last apparently all hand-work. But it is head-work and heart-work too, and the men who wrought at it wrought with such intensity and constancy that they did not once look up or round where we paused to look on. I was made to know that trade was dull and work slack, and these fellows were lucky fellows to have anything to do. Still I did not envy them; and I felt it a distinct relief to pass from their shops into the cool, dim crypt which was filled with tusks of ivory, in all sizes from those of the largest father elephant to those of the babes of the herd; these were milk-tusks, I suppose. They get dearer as the elephants get scarcer; and that must have been why I paid as much for a penknife in the glittering showroom as it would have cost me in New York, with the passage money and the duties added. Because of the price, perhaps, I did not think of buying the two-thousand-bladed penknife I saw there; but I could never have used all the blades, now that we no longer make quill pens. I looked fondly at the maker's name on the knife I did buy, and said that the table cutlery of a certain small household which set itself up forty years ago had borne the same: but the pleasant salesman did not seem to feel the pathos of the fact so much as I.

W. D. Howells

IV

There is not only a vast deal of industry in Sheffield, but there is an unusual abundance of history, as there might very well be in a place that began life, in the usual English fashion, under the Britons and grew into municipal consciousness in the fostering care of the Romans and the ruder nurture of the Saxons, Danes, and Normans. Lords it had of the last, and the great line of the Earls of Shrewsbury presently rose and led Sheffield men back to battle in France, where the first earl fell on the bloody field, and so many of the men died with him in 1453 that there was not a house in all the region which did not mourn a loss. Which of the Roses Sheffield held for, White or Red, I am not sure; but we will say that it duly suffered for one or the other; and it is certain that the great Cardinal Wolsey rested eighteen days at Sheffield Manor just before he went to die at Leicester; and Mary Queen of Scots spent fourteen years of sorrowful captivity, sometimes at the Manor and sometimes in Sheffield Castle. This hold was taken by the Parliamentarians in the Civil War; but the famous industries of the place had begun long before; so that Chaucer could say of one of his pilgrims,

"A Sheffield thwytel bare he in his hose."

Thwytels, or whittles, figured in the broils and stage-plays of Elizabethan times, and three gross of them were exported from Liverpool in 1589, when the Sheffield penknife was already famed the best in the world. Manufactures flourished there apace when England turned to them from agriculture, and Sheffield is now a city of four hundred thousand or more. Apparently it has been growing radical, as the centres of prosperity and adversity always do, and the days of the Chartist agitation continued there for ten years, from 1839 till it came as near open rebellion as it well could in a plot for an armed uprising. Then that cause of the people, like many another, failed, and liberty there, as elsewhere in England, was fain to

"broaden slowly down   From precedent to precedent."

Labor troubles, patient or violent, have followed, as labor troubles must, but leisure has always been equal to their pacification, and now Sheffield takes its adversity almost as quietly as its prosperity.

W. D. Howells

V

We were not there, though, for others' labor or leisure, which we have plenty of at home; but even before I appeased such conscience as I had about seeing a type of the works, we went a long drive up out of the town to that Manor where the poor, brilliant, baddish Scotch queen was imprisoned by her brilliant, baddish English cousin. In any question of goodness, there was little to choose between them; both were blood-stained liars; but it is difficult being a good woman and a queen too, and they only failed where few have triumphed. Mary is the more appealing to the fancy because she suffered beyond her deserts, but Elizabeth was to be pitied because Mary had made it politically imperative for her to kill her. All this we had threshed out many times before, and had said that, cat for cat, Mary was the more dangerous because she was the more feminine, and Elizabeth the more detestable because she was the more masculine in her ferocity. We were therefore in the right mood to visit Mary's prison, and we were both indignant and dismayed to find that our driver, called from a mews at a special price set upon his intelligence, had never heard of it and did not know where it was.

We reported his inability to the head porter, who came out of the hotel in a fine flare of sarcasm. "You call yourself a Sheffield man and not know where the Old Manor is!" he began, and presently reduced that proud ignoramus of a driver to such a willingness to learn that we thought it at least safe to set out with him, and so started for the long climb up the hills that hold Sheffield in their hollow. When we reached their crest, we looked down and back through the clearer air upon as strange and grand a sight as could be. It was as if we were looking into the crater of a volcano, which was sending up its smoke through a thousand vents. All detail of the works and their chimneys was lost in the retrospect; one was aware only of a sort of sea of vapor through which they loomed and gloomed.

Our ascent was mostly through winding and climbing streets of little dirty houses, with frowsy gardens beside them, and the very dirtiest-faced children in England playing about them. From time to time our driver had to ask his way of the friendly flat- bosomed slatterns, with babies in their arms, on their thresholds, or the women tending shop, or peddling provisions, who were all kind to him, and assured him with varying degrees of confidence that the Old Manor was a bit, or a goodish bit, beyond. All at once we came upon the sight of it on an open top, hard by what is left of the ruins of the real Manor, where Wolsey stayed that little while from death. The relics are broken walls, higher here, lower there; with some Tudor fireplaces showing through their hollow windows. What we saw in tolerable repair was the tower of the Manor, or the lodge, and we drove to it across a field, on a track made by farm carts, and presently kept by a dog that showed his teeth in a grin not wholly of amusement at our temerity. While we debated whether we had not better let the driver get down and knock, a farmer-like man came to the door and called the dog off. Then, in a rich North Country accent, he welcomed us to his kitchen parlor, where his wife was peeling potatoes for their midday dinner, and so led us up the narrow stone stairs of the tower to the chambers where Mary miserably passed those many long years of captivity.

The rooms were visibly restored in every point where they could have needed restoration, but they were not ruthlessly or too insistently restored. There was even an antique chair, but when our guide was put on his honor as to whether it was one of the original chairs he answered, "Well, if people wanted a chair!" He was a rather charmingly quaint,

W. D. Howells

humorous person, with that queer conscience, and he did not pretend to be moved by the hard inexorable stoniness of the place which had been a queen's prison for many years. One must not judge it too severely, though: bowers and prisons of that day looked much alike, and Mary Stuart may have felt this a bower, and only hated it because she could not get out of it, or anyhow break the relentless hold of that Earl and Countess of Shrewsbury whose captive guest she was, though she never ceased trying. We went up on the wide flat roof, of lead or stone, whither her feet must have so often heavily climbed, and looked out over the lovely landscape which she must have abhorred; and the wind that blew over it, in late August, was very cold; far colder than the air of the prison, or the bower, below.

The place belongs now to the Duke of Norfolk, the great Catholic duke, and owes its restoration to his pity and his piety. Our farmer guide was himself a Protestant, but he spoke well of the duke, with whom he reported himself in such colloquies as, "I says to Dook," and, "Dook says to me." When he understood that we were Americans he asked after a son of his who had gone out to our continent twenty years before. He had only heard from him once, and that on the occasion of his being robbed of all his money by a roommate. It was in a place called Massatusy; we suggested Massachusetts, and he assented that such might be the place; and Mary's prison-house acquired an added pathos.

VI

We drove back through the beautiful park, the Duke of Norfolk's gift to Sheffield, which is plentifully provided, like all English towns, with public pleasure-grounds. They lie rather outside of it, but within it are many and many religious and civic edifices which merit to be seen. We chose as chiefest the ancient Parish Church, of Norman origin and modern restoration, where we visited the tomb of the Lord and Lady Shrewsbury who were Mary Stuart's jailers; or if they were not, a pair of their family were, and it comes to the same thing, emotionally. The chapel in which they lie is most beautiful, and the verger had just brushed the carpet within the chancel to such immaculate dustlessness that he could not bring himself to let us walk over it. He let us walk round it, and we saw the chapel as a favor, which we discharged with an abnormal tip after severe debate whether a person of this verger's rich respectability and perfect manner would take any tip at all. In the event it appeared that he would.

*   *   *   *   *

W. D. Howells

NINE DAYS' WONDER IN YORK

Perhaps it would be better to come to York somewhat earlier in the year than the 2d of September. By that time the English summer has suffered often if not severe discouragements. It has really only two months out of the year to itself, and even July and August are not always constant to it. To be sure, their defection cannot spoil it, but they dispose it to the slights of September in a dejection from which there is no rise to those coquetries with October known to our own summer. Yet, having said so much, I feel bound to add that our nine days in York, from the 2d to the 12th of September, were more summer than autumn days, some wholly, some partly, with hours of sunshine keeping the flowers bright which the rain kept fresh. If you walked fast in this sunshine you were quite hot, and sometimes in the rain you were uncomfortably warm, or at least you were wet. If the mornings demanded a fire in the grate, the evenings were so clement that the lamp was sufficient, and the noons were very well with neither.

I

The day of our arrival in York began bright at Sheffield, where there was a man quarrelling so loudly and aimlessly in the station that we were glad to get away from him, as well as from the mountains of slag surrounding the iron metropolis. The train ran through a pass in these, and then we found ourselves in a plain country, and, though the day turned gray and misty, there seemed a sort of stored sunshine in the fields of wheat which the farmers were harvesting far and near. One has heard so much of the decay of the English agriculture that one sees what is apparently the contrary with nothing less than astonishment. The acreage of these wheatfields was large, and the yield heavier than I could remember to have seen at home. Where the crop had been got in, much ploughing for the next year had been done already, and where the ploughing was finished the work of sowing by drill was going steadily forward, in the faith that such an unprecedented summer as was now passing would return another year. At all these pleasant labors, of course, the rooks were helping, or at least bossing.

W. D. Howells

II

We expected to stay certainly a week, and perhaps two weeks, in York, and our luck with railway hotels had been so smiling elsewhere that we had no other mind than to spend the time at the house into which we all but stepped from our train. But we had reckoned without our host, as he was represented by one of a half-dozen alert young ladies in the office, who asked how long we expected to stay, and when we expressed a general purpose of staying indefinitely, said that all her rooms were taken from the next Monday by people who had engaged them long before for the races. I did not choose to betray my ignorance to a woman, but I privately asked the head porter what races those were which were limiting our proposed sojourn, and I am now afraid he had some difficulty in keeping a head porter's conventional respect for a formal superior in answering that we had arrived on the eve of Doncaster Week. Then I said, "Oh yes," and affected the knowledge of Doncaster Week which I resolved to acquire by staying somewhere in York till it was over.

But as yet, that Friday afternoon, there was no hurry, and, instead of setting about a search for lodgings at once, we drove up into the town, as soon as we had tea, and visited York Minster while it was still the gray afternoon and not yet the gray evening. I thought the hour fortunate, and I do not see yet how we could have chosen a better hour out of the whole twenty-four, for the inside or the outside of the glorious fane, the grandest and beautifulest in all England, as I felt then and I feel now. If I were put to the question and were forced to say in what its supreme grandeur and beauty lay, I should perhaps say in its most ample simplicity. No doubt it is full of detail, but I keep no sense of this from that mighty interior, with its tree-like, clustered pillars, and its measureless windows, like breadths of stained foliage in autumnal woodlands. You want the scale of nature for the Minster at York, and I cannot liken it to less than all-out-doors. Some cathedrals, like that of Wells, make you think of gardens; but York Minster will not be satisfied with less than an autumnal woodland, where the trees stand in clumps, with grassy levels about them, and with spacious openings to the sky, that let in the colored evening light.

You could not get lost in it, for it was so free of all such architectural undergrowth as cumbers the perspectives of some cathedrals; besides, the afternoon of our visit there were so many other Americans that you could easily have asked your way in your own dialect. We loitered over its lengths and breadths, and wondered at its windows, which were like the gates of sunrise and sunset for magnitude, and lingered in a sumptuous delay from going into the choir, delighting in the gray twilight which seemed to gather from the gray walls inward, when suddenly what seemed a metallic curtain was dropped with a clash and the simultaneous up-flashing of electric bulbs inside it, and we were shut out from the sight but not the sound of the service that began in the choir. We could not wholly regret the incident, for as we recalled the like operation of religion in churches of our Italian travel, we were reminded how equally authoritative the Church of England and the Church of Home were, and how little they adjust their ceremonial to the individual, how largely to the collective worshipper. You could come into the Minster of York as into the basilica of St. Mark at Venice for a silent prayer amid the religious influences of the place, and be conscious of your oneness with your Source, as if there were no other one; but when the priesthood called you as one of many to your devotions, it was with the same imperative voice in both, and you must obey or be cut off from your chance. I suppose it is right; but somehow the down-clashing of that screen of the choir in the

W. D. Howells

Minster at York seemed to exclude us with reproach, almost with ignominy.

We did what we could to repair our wounded self respect, and did not lay our exclusion up against the Minster itself, which I find that I noted as "scatteringly noble outside." By this I dare say I meant it had not that artistic unity of which I brought the impression from the inside. They were doing, as they were always doing, every where, with English cathedrals, something to one of the towers; but this only enhanced its scattering nobleness, for it left that greatly bescaffolded tower largely to the imagination, in which it soared sublimer, if anything, than its compeer. Most of the streets leading to and from the rather insufficient, irregular square where the Minster stands are lanes of little houses of the fifteenth and sixteenth, centuries, which collectively curved in their line, and not only overhung at their second stories, but bulged outward involuntarily from the weakness of age. They were all quite habitable, and some much later dwellings immediately surrounding the church were the favorite sojourn, apparently, of such strangers as could have rooms at the hotels only until the Monday of Doncaster Week.

III

During those limited days of the week before Doncaster, I was constantly coming back to the Minster, which is not the germ of political York, or hardly religious York; the brave city was a Romano-British capital and a Romano-British episcopal see centuries before the first wooden temple was built on the site of the present edifice in 627. I should like to make believe that we found traces of that simple church in the crypt of the Minster when we went the next morning and were herded through it by the tenderest of vergers. Most of our flock were Americans, and we put our guide to such question in matters of imagination and information as the patience of a less amiable shepherd would not have borne. Many a tale, true or o'ertrue, our verger had, which he told with unction; when he ascended with us to the body of the church, and said that the stained glass of the gigantic windows suffered from the depredations of the mistaken birds which pecked holes in the joints of their panes, I felt that I had full measure from him, pressed down and running over. I do not remember why he said the birds should have done this, but it seems probable that they took the mellow colors of the glass for those of ripe fruits.

For myself, I could not get enough of those windows, in another sort of famine which ought at this time to have been sated. I was forever wondering at their grandeur outside and their glory inside. I was glad to lose my way about the town, for if I kept walking I was sure, sooner or later, to bring up at the Minster; but the last evening of our stay I made a purposed pilgrimage to it for a final emotion. It was the clearest evening we had in York, and at half-past six the sun was setting in a transparent sky, which somehow it did not flush with any of those glaring reds which the vulgarer sorts of sunsets are fond of, but bathed the air in a delicate

W. D. Howells

suffusion of daffodil light, just tinged with violet. This was the best medium to see the past of the Minster in, and I can see it there now, if I did not then. I followed, or I follow, its veracious history back to the beginning of the seventh century, whence you can look back further still to the earliest Christian temples where the Romans worshipped with the Britons, whom they had enslaved and converted. But it was not till 627 that the little wooden chapel was built on the site of the Minster, to house the rite of the Northumbrian King Eadwine's baptism. He felt so happy in his new faith that he replaced the wooden structure with stone. In the next century it was burned, but rebuilt by another pious prince, and probably repaired by yet another after the Danes took the city a hundred years later. It was then in a good state to be destroyed by that devout William the Conqueror, who came to take the Saxon world in its sins of guttling and guzzling. The first Norman archbishop reconstructed or restored the church, and then it began to rise and to spread in glory— nave, transepts, and choir, and pillars and towers, Norman and Early English, and Perpendicular and Decorated—till it found itself at last what the American tourist sees it to-day. It suffered from two great fires in the nineteenth century, the first set by a lunatic who had the fancy of seeing it burn, but who had only the satisfaction of destroying part of the roof.

It was never richly painted, but the color wanting in the walls and fretted vault was more than compensated by the mellowed splendors of the matchless windows. It was, indeed, fit to be the home of much more secular history than can be associated with it; but not till the end of the thirteenth century had the Minster a patron of its own, when St. William was canonized, and exercised his office, whatever it was, for two brief centuries. Then the Cromwell of Henry VIII. took possession of it in behalf of the crown, and the saint's charge was practically abolished. He was even deprived of his head, for the relic was encased in gold and jewels, and was therefore worth the king's having, who was most a friend of the reformed religion when it paid best. The later Cromwell, who beat a later king hard by at Marston Moor, must have somehow desecrated the Minster, though there is no record of any such fact. A more authentic monument of the religious difficulties of the times is the pastoral staff, bearing the arms of Catharine of Braganza, the poor little wife of Charles II., which was snatched from a Roman Catholic bishop when, to the high offence of Protestant piety, he was heading a procession in York in 1688. The verger showing us through the Minster was a good Protestant, but he held it bad taste in a predecessor of his, who when leading about a Catholic party of sight-seers took the captive staff from its place and shook it in their faces, saying, "Don't you wish you had it?"

W. D. Howells

IV

There is no telling to what lengths true religion, may rightly not go. I rather prize the incident as the sole fact concerning the Minster which I could make sure of even after repeated visits, and if I am indebted for my associations with it, long after the event, to Dr. Raine's scholarly and interesting sketch of York history, there is no reason why the better-informed reader should not accompany me in my last visit fully equipped. I walked slowly all round the structure, and fancied that I got a new sense of grandeur in the effect of the east window, which was, at any rate, more impressive than the north window. It was a long walk, almost the measure of such a walk as one should take after supper for one's health, and it had such incidents as many pauses for staring up at the many restorations going on. From point to point the incomparable Perpendicular Gothic carried the eye to the old gargoyles of the caves and towers waiting to be replaced by the new gargoyles, which lay in open-mouthed grimacing in the grass at the bases of the church. While I stood noting both, and thinking the chances were that I should never look on York Minster again, and feeling the luxurious pang of it, a verger in a skull-cap was so good as to come to a side door and parley long and pleasantly with a policeman. The simple local life went on around; people going to or from supper passed me; kind, vulgar noises came from the little houses bulging over the narrow, neighboring streets; there seemed to be the stamping of horses in a stable, and there was certainly the misaspirated talk about them. I could not have asked better material for the humble emotions I love; and I was more than content on my way home to find myself one of the congregation at the loud devotions of a detachment of the Salvation Army. After a battering of drums and a clashing of cymbals and a shouting of hymns, the worship settled to the prayer of a weak brother, who was so long in supplication that the head exhorter covered a yawn with his hand, and at the first sign of relenting in the supplicant bade the drums and cymbals strike up. Then, after a hymn, a sister, such a very plain, elderly sister, with hardly a tooth or an aitch in her head, began to relate her religious history. It appeared that she had been a much greater sinner than she looked, and that the mercy shown her had been proportionate. She was vain both of her sins and mercies, poor soul, and in her scrimp figure, with its ill-fitting uniform, Heaven knows how long she went on. I was distracted by a clergyman passing on the outside of the ring of listening women and children, and looking, I chose to think, somewhat sourly askance at the distasteful ceremonial. I wished to stop him, on his way to the Minster, if that was his way, and tell him that so Christianity must have begun, and so the latest form of it must always begin and work round after ages and ages to the beauty and respectability his own ritual has. But I now believe this would have been the greatest impertinence and hypocrisy, for I myself found the performance before us as tasteless and tawdry as he could possibly have done. He was going toward the Minster, and it would make him forget it; but I was going away from it, perhaps, for the last time, and this loud side-show of religion would make me forget the Minster.

W. D. Howells

V

Our railway hotel lay a little way out of the town, and after a day's sight-seeing we were to meet or mingle with troops of wholesome-looking workmen whose sturdiness and brightness were a consolation after the pale debility of labor's looks in Sheffield. From the chocolate-factories or the railroad-shops, which are the chief industries of York, they would be crossing the bridge of the Ouse, the famous stream on which the Romans had their town, and which suggested to the Anglicans to call their Eboracum Eurewic—a town on a river. In due time the Danes modified this name to Yerik, and so we came honestly by the name of our own New York, called after the old York, as soon as the English had robbed the Dutch of it, and the King of England had given the province to his brother the Duke of York. Both cities are still towns on rivers, but the Ouse is no more an image or forecast of the Hudson than Old York is of New York. For that reason, the bridge over it is not to be compared to our Brooklyn Bridge, or even to any bridge which is yet to span the Hudson. The difference is so greatly in our favor that we may well yield our city's mother the primacy in her city wall. We have ourselves as yet no Plantagenet wall, and we have not yet got a mediaeval gate through which the traveller passes in returning from the Flatiron Building to his hotel in the Grand Central Station.

We do not begin to have such a hoar antiquity as is articulate in the mother city, speaking with muted voices from the innumerable monuments which the earth has yielded from the site of our hotel and its adjacent railway station. All underground York is doubtless fuller of Home than even Bath is; and it has happened that her civilization was much more largely dug up here than elsewhere when the foundations of the spreading edifices were laid. The relics are mainly the witnesses of pagan Rome, but Christianity politically began in York, as it has politically ended in New York, and doubtless some soldiers of the Sixth Legion and many of the British slaves were religiously Christians in the ancient metropolis before Constantine was elected emperor there.

I have been in many places where history is hospitably at home and is not merely an unwilling guest, as in our unmemoried land. Florence is very well, Venice is not so bad, Naples has her long thoughts, and Milan is mediaeval-minded, not to speak of Genoa, or Marseilles, or Paris, or those romantic German towns where the legends, if not the facts, abound; but, after all, for my pleasure in the past, I could not choose any place before York. You need not be so very definite in your knowledge. The event of Constantine's presence and election is so spacious as to leave no room for particulars in the imagination; and you are so rich in it that you will even reject them from your thoughts, as you sit in the close-cropped flowery lawn of your hotel garden (try to imagine a railroad hotel garden in *New* York!) on the sunniest of the afternoons before you are turned out for Doncaster Week, and, while you watch a little adventurous American boy climbing over a pile of rock-work, realize the most august, the most important fact in the story of the race as native to the very air you are breathing! Where you sit you are in full view of the Minster, which is to say in view of something like the towers and battlements of the celestial city. Or if you wake very early on a morning still nearer the fatal Doncaster Week of your impending banishment, and look out of your lofty windows at the sunrise reddening the level bars of cloud behind the Minster, you shall find it bulked up against the pearl-gray masses of the sunny mist which hangs in all the intervening trees, and solidifies them in unbroken masses of foliage. All round your hotel spreads a gridiron of railroad, yet such is the force of the English

W. D. Howells

genius for quiet that you hear no clatter of trains; the expresses whir in and out of the station with not more noise than humming-birds; and amid this peace the past has some chance with modernity. The Britons dwell, unmolested by our latter-day clamor, in their wattled huts and dugouts; the Romans come and make them slaves and then Christians, and after three or four hundred years send word from the Tiber to the Ouse that they can stay no longer, and so leave them naked to their enemies, the Picts and Scots and Saxons and Angles; and in due course come the ravaging and burning Danes; and in due course still, the murdering and plundering and scorning Normans. But all so quietly, like the humming-bird-like expresses, with a kind of railway celerity in the foreshortened retrospect; and after the Normans have crushed themselves down into the mass of the vanquished, and formed the English out of the blend, there follow the many wars of the successions, of the Roses, of the Stuarts, with all the intermediate insurrections and rebellions. In the splendid Histories of Shakespeare, which are full of York, the imagination visits and revisits the place, and you are entreated by mouth of one of his princely personages,

"I pray you let us satisfy our eyes
With the memorials and things of fame,
That do renown this city,"

where his Henrys and Richards and Margarets and Edwards and Eleanors abide still and shall forever abide while the English speech lasts.

VI

Something of all this I knew, and more pretended, with a
mounting indignation at the fast-coming Doncaster Week
which was to turn us out of our hotel. We began our search
for other lodgings with what seemed to be increasing failure.
The failure had consolation in it so far as the sweet regret of
people whose apartments were taken could console. They
would have taken us at other hotels for double the usual
price, but, when we showed ourselves willing to pay, it
proved that they had no rooms at any price. From house to
house, then, we went, at first vaingloriously, in the spaces
about the Minster, and then meekly into any side street,
wherever the legend of Apartments showed itself in a
transom. At last, the second day, after being denied at seven
successive houses, we found quite the refuge we wanted in
the Bootham, which means very much more than the
ignorant reader can imagine. Our upper rooms looked on a
pretty grassy garden space behind, where there was sun
when there was sun, and in front on the fine old brick
dwellings of a most personable street, with a sentiment of
bygone fashion. At the upper end of it was a famous city
gate—Bootham Bar, namely—with a practicable portcullis,
which we verified at an early moment by going up into "the
chamber over the gate," where it was once worked, and
whence its lower beam, set thick with savage spikes, was
dropped. Outside the gate there was a sign in the wall saying
that guards were to be had there to guide travellers through
the Forest of Galtres beyond Bootham, and keep them from
the wolves. Now woods and wolves and guards are all gone,
and Bootham Bar is never closed.

The upper room is a passageway for people who are walking
round the town on the Plantagenet wall, and one morning we
took this walk in sunshine that befitted the Sabbath. Half the

W. D. Howells

children of York seemed to be taking it, too, with their good parents, who had stayed away from church to give them this pleasure, the fathers putting on their frock-coats and top-hats, which are worn on no other days in the provincial cities of England. For a Plantagenet wall, that of York is in excellent repair, and it is very clean, so that the children could not spoil their Sunday best by clambering on the parapet, and trying to fall over it. There was no parapet on the other side, and they could have fallen over that without trouble; but it would not have served the same purpose; for under the parapet there were the most alluringly ragged little boys, with untidy goats and delightfully dirty geese. There was no trace of a moat outside the wall, where pleasant cottages pressed close to it with their gardens full of bright flowers. At one point there were far-spreading sheep and cattle pens, where there is a weekly market, and at another the old Norman castle which cruel Conqueror William built to hold the city, and which has suffered change, not unpicturesque, into prisons for unluckier criminals, and the Assize Courts for their condemnation. From time to time the wall left off, and then we got down, perforce, and walked to the next piece of it. In these pieces we made the most of the old gates, especially Walmgate Bar, which has a barbican. I should be at a loss to say why the barbican should have commended it so; perhaps it was because we there realized, for the first time, what a barbican was; I doubt if the reader knows, now. Otherwise, I should have preferred Monk Bar or Micklegate Bar, as being more like those I was used to in the theatre. But we came back gladly to Bootham Bar, holding that a portcullis was equal any day to a barbican, and feeling as if we had got home in the more familiar neighborhood.

There were small shops in the Bootham, thread-and-needle stores, newspaper stores, and provision stores mainly, which I affected, and there was one united florist's and fruiterer's which I particularly liked because of the conversability of the proprietor. He was a stout man, of a vinous complexion, with what I should call here, where our speech is mostly uncouth, an educated accent, though with few and wandering aspirates in it. Him I visited every morning to buy for my breakfast one of those Spanish melons which they have everywhere in England, and which put our native cantaloupes to shame; and we always fell into a little talk over our transaction of fourpence or sixpence, as the case might be. After I had confided that I was an American, he said one day, "Ah, the Americans are clever people." Then he added, "I hope you won't mind my saying it, sir, but I think their ladies are rather harder than our English ladies, sir."

"Yes," I eagerly assented. "How do you mean? Sharper? Keener?"

"Well, not just that, sir."

"More practical? More business-like?" I pursued.

"Well, I shouldn't like to say that, sir. But—they seem rather harder, sir; at least, judging from what I see of them in York, sir. Rather harder, sir."

We remained not the less friends with that mystery between us; and I bought my last melon of him on my last morning, when the early September had turned somewhat sharply chill. That turn made me ask what the winter was in York, and he boasted it very cold, with ice and snow aplenty, and degrees of frost much like our own. But apparently those York women resisted it and remained of a tenderness which contrasted to their advantage with the summer hardness of our women.

VII

It was a pleasure, which I should be glad to share with the reader, to lose one's self in the streets of York. They were all kinds of streets except straight, and they seemed not to go anywhere except for the joke of bringing the wayfarer unexpectedly back to, or near, his starting-point and far from his goal. The blame of their vagariousness, if it was a fault, is put upon the Danes, who found York when they captured it very rectangular, for so the Romans built it, and so the Angles kept it; but nothing would serve the Danes but to crook its streets and call them gates, so that the real gates of the city have to be called bars, or else the stranger might take them for streets. If he asked another wayfarer, he could sometimes baffle the streets, and get to the point he aimed at, but, whether he did or not, he could always amuse himself in them; they would take a friendly interest in him, and show him the old houses and churches which the American stranger prefers. They abound in the poorer sorts of buildings, of course, just as they do in the poorer sorts of people, but in their simpler courts and squares and expanses they have often dignified mansions of that Georgian architecture which seems the last word in its way, and which is known here in our older edifices as there in their newer. Some of them are said to have "richly carved ceilings, wainscoted, panelled rooms, chimneypieces with paintings framed in the over-mantel, dentilled cornices, and pedimented doors," and I could well believe it, as I passed them with an envious heart. There were gardens behind these mansions which hung their trees over the spiked coping of their high-shouldered walls and gates, and sequestered I know not what damp social events in their flowery and leafy bounds.

At times I distinctly wished to know something of the life of

York, but I was not in the way of it. The nearest to an acquaintance I had there, besides my critical fruiterer, was the actor whose name I recognized on his bills as that of a brave youth who had once dramatized a novel of mine, and all too briefly played the piece, and who was now to come to York for a week of Shakespeare. Perhaps I could not forgive him the recrudescence; at any rate, I did not try to see him, and there was no other social chance for me, except as I could buy in for a few glimpses at the tidy confectioners', where persons of civil condition resorted for afternoon tea. Even to these one could not speak, and I could only do my best in a little mercenary conversation with the bookseller about York histories. The book- stores were not on our scale, and generally the shops in York were not of the modern department type, but were perhaps the pleasanter for that reason.

In my earlier wanderings I made the acquaintance of a most agreeable market-place, stretching the length of two squares, which on a Saturday afternoon I found filled with every manner of bank and booth and canopied counter, three deep, and humming pleasantly with traffic in everything one could eat, drink, wear, or read; there seemed as many book-stalls as fruit-stalls. What I noted equally with the prettiness of the abounding flowers was the mild kindness of the market-people's manners and their extreme anxiety to state exactly the quality of the things they had for sale. They seemed incapable of deceit, but I do not say they really were so. My own transactions were confined to the purchase of some golden-gage plums, and I advise the reader rather to buy greengages; the other plums practised the deception in their looks which their venders abhorred.

VIII

I wandered in a perfectly contemporary mood through the long ranks and lanes of the marketplace, and did not know till afterward that at one end of it, called the Pavement, the public executions used to take place for those great or small occasions which brought folks to the block or scaffold in the past. I had later some ado to verify the dismal fact from a cluster of people before a tavern who seemed to be taking bets for the Doncaster Week, and I could hardly keep them from booking me for this horse or that when I merely wanted to know whether it was on a certain spot the Earl of Northumberland had his head cut off for leading a rising against Henry IV.; or some such execution.

What riches of story has not York to browbeat withal the storyless New-Yorker who visits her! That Henry IV. was he whom I had lately seen triumphing near Shrewsbury in the final battle of the Roses, where the Red was so bloodily set above the White; and it was his poetic fancy to have Northumberland, when he bade him come to York, pass through the gateway on which the head of his son, Hotspur Harry, was festering. No wonder the earl led a rising against his liege, who had first mercifully meant to imprison him for life, and then more mercifully pardoned him. But there seems to have been fighting up and down the centuries from the beginning, in York, interspersed with praying and wedding and feasting. After the citizens drove out Conqueror William's garrison, and Earl Waltheof provided against the Normans' return by standing at the castle gate and chopping their heads off with his battle-axe as they came forth, William efficaciously devastated the city and the country as far as Durham. His son William gave it a church, and that "worthy peer," King Stephen, a hospital. In his time the archbishop and barons of York beat the Scotch hard by, and the next Scotch king had to do homage to Henry II. at York for his kingdom. Henry III. married his sister at York to one Scotch king and his daughter to that king's successor. Edward I. and his queen Eleanor honored with their presence the translation of St. William's bones to the Minster; Edward II. retreated from his defeat at Bannockburn to York, and Edward III. was often there for a king's varied occasions of fighting and feasting. Weak Henry VI. and his wilful Margaret, after their defeat at Towton by Edward IV., escaped from the city just in time, and Edward entered York under his own father's head on Micklegate Bar. Richard III. was welcomed there before his rout and death at Bosworth, and was truly mourned by the citizens. Henry VII. wedded Elizabeth, the "White Rose of York," and afterward visited her city; Mary, Queen of Scots, was once in hiding there, and her uncouth son stayed two nights in York on his way to be crowned James I. in London. His son, Charles I., was there early in his reign, and touched many for the king's evil; later, he was there again, but could not cure the sort of king's evil which raged past all magic in the defeat of his followers at Marston Moor by Cromwell. The city yielded to the Puritans, whose temperament had already rather characterized it. James II., as Duke of York, made it his brief sojourn; "proud Cumberland," returning from Culloden after the defeat of the Pretender, visited the city and received its freedom for destroying the last hope of the Stuarts; perhaps the twenty-two rebels who were then put to death in York were executed in the very square where those wicked men thought I was wanting to play the horses. The reigning family has paid divers visits to the ancient metropolis, which was the capital of Britain before London was heard of. The old prophecy of her ultimate primacy must make time if it is to fulfil itself and increase York's seventy-two thousand beyond London's six million.

W. D. Howells

IX

I should be at a loss to say why its English memories
haunted my York less than the Roman associations of the
place. They form, however, rather a clutter of incidents,
whereas the few spreading facts of Hadrian's stay, the deaths
of Severus and Constantius, and the election of Constantine,
his son, enlarge themselves to the atmospheric compass of
the place, but leave a roominess in which the fancy may
more commodiously orb about. I was on terms of more
neighborly intimacy with the poor Punic emperor than with
any one else in York, doubtless because, when he fell sick,
he visited the temple of Bellona near Bootham Bar, and paid
his devotions unmolested, let us hope, by any prevision of
the misbehavior of his son Caracalla (whose baths I had long
ago visited at Rome) in killing his other son Geta. Everywhere I could be an early Christian, in company with
Constantine, in whom the instinct of political Christianity
must have begun to stir as soon as he was chosen emperor.
But I dare say I heard the muted tramp of the Sixth Legion
about the Yorkish streets above all other martial sounds
because I stayed as long as Doncaster Week would let me in
the railway hotel, which so many of their bones made room
for when the foundations of it were laid, with those of the
adherent station. Their bones seem to have been left there,
after the disturbance, but their sepulchres were respectfully
transferred to the museum of the Philosophical Society, in
the grounds where the ruins of St. Mary's Abbey rise like
fragments of pensive music or romantic verse, inviting the
moonlight and the nightingale, but, wanting these, make shift
with the noonday and the babies in perambulators neglected
by nurse-girls reading novels.

The babies and the nurses are not allowed in the museum of
antiquities, which is richer in Roman remains than any that

one sees outside of Italy. There are floors of mosaic, large and perfect, taken from the villas which people are always digging up in the neighborhood of York, and, from the graves uncovered in the railway excavations, coffins of lead and stone for civilians, and of rude tiles for the soldiers of the Sixth Legion; the slaves were cast into burial-pits of tens and twenties and left to indiscriminate decay till they should be raised in the universal incorruption. Probably the slaves were the earliest Christians at York; certainly the monuments are pagan, as the inmates of the tombs must have been. Some of the monuments bear inscriptions from loving wives and husbands to the partners they have lost, and some of the stone coffins are those of children. It is all infinitely touching, and after two thousand years the heart aches for the fathers and mothers who laid their little ones away in these hard cradles for their last sleep. Faith changes, but constant death remains the same, and life is not very different in any age, when it comes to the end. The Roman exiles who had come so far to hold my British ancestors in subjection to their alien rule seemed essentially not only of the same make as me, but the same civilization. Their votive altars and inscriptions to other gods expressed a human piety of like anxiety and helplessness with ours, and called to a like irresponsive sky. A hundred witnesses of their mortal state—jars and vases and simple household utensils—fill the shelves of the museum; but the most awful, the most beautiful appeal of the past is in that mass of dark auburn hair which is kept here in a special urn and uncovered for your supreme emotion. It is equally conjectured to be the hair of a Roman lady or of a British princess, but is of a young girl certainly, dressed twenty centuries ago for the tomb in which it was found, and still faintly lucent with the fashionable unguent of the day, and kept in form by pins of jet. One thinks of the little, slender hands that used to put them there, and of the eyes that confronted themselves in the silver mirror under the warm shadow that the red-gold mass cast upon the white forehead. This sanctuary of the past was the most interesting place in that most interesting city of York, and the day of our first visit a princess of New York sat reading a book in the midst of it, waiting for the rain to be over, which was waiting for her to come out and then begin again. We knew her from having seen her at the station in relation to some trunks bearing her initials and those of her native city; and she could be about the age of the York princess or young Roman lady whose hair was kept in the urn hard by.

X

There is in York a little, old, old church, whose dear and reverend name I have almost forgotten, if ever I knew it, but I think it is Holy Trinity Goodramgate, which divides the heart of my adoration with the Minster. We came to it quite by accident, one of our sad September afternoons, after we had been visiting the Guildhall, Venetianly overhanging the canal calm of the Ouse, and very worthy to be seen for its York histories in stained glass. The custodian had surprised us and the gentlemen of the committee by taking us into the room where they were investigating the claims of the registered voters to the suffrage; and so, much entertained and instructed, we issued forth, and, passing by the church in which Guy Fawkes was baptized, only too ineffectually, we came quite unexpectedly upon Holy Trinity Goodramgate, if that and not another is indeed its name.

It stands sequestered in a little leafy and grassy space of its own, with a wall hardly overlooked on one side by low stone cottages, the immemorial homes of rheumatism and influenza. The church had the air of not knowing that it is of Perpendicular and Decorated Gothic, with a square, high-shouldered tower, as it bulks up to a very humble height from the turf to the boughs overhead, or that it has a nice girl sketching its doorway, where a few especially favored weddings and funerals may enter. It is open once a year for service, and when the tourist will, or can, for the sight of the time-mellowed, beautiful stained glass of its eastward window. The oaken pews are square and high- shouldered, like the low church tower; and, without, the soft yellow sandstone is crumbling away from the window traceries. The church did not look as if it felt itself a thousand years old, and perhaps it is not; but I never was in a place where I seemed so like a ghost of that antiquity. I had a sense of haunting it, in the inner twilight and the outer sunlight, where a tender wind was stirring the leaves of its embowering trees and scattering them on the graves of my eleventh and twelfth century contemporaries.

XI

We chose the sunniest morning we could for our visit to Clifford's Tower, which remains witness of the Norman castle the Conqueror built and rebuilt to keep the Danish-Anglian-Roman- British town in awe. But the tower was no part of the original castle, and only testifies of it by hearsay. That was built by Roger de Clifford, who suffered death with his party chief, the Earl of Lancaster, when Edward of York took the city, and it is mainly memorable as the refuge of the Jews whom the Christians had harried out of their homes. They had grown in numbers and riches, when the Jew-hate of 1190 broke out in England, as from time to time the Jew-hate breaks out in Russia now, to much the same cruel effect. They were followed and besieged in the castle, and, seeing that they must be captured, they set fire to the place, and five hundred slew themselves. Some that promised to be Christians came out and were killed by their brethren in Christ. In New York the Christians have grown milder, and now they only keep the Jews out of their clubs and their homes.

The Clifford Tower leans very much to one side, so that as you ascend it for the magnificent view from the top you have to incline yourself the other way, as you do in the Tower of Pisa, to help it keep its balance. The morning of our visit, so gay in its forgetfulness of the tragical past, we found the place in charge of an old soldier, an Irishman who had learned, as custodian, a professional compassion for those poor Jews of nine hundred years ago, and, being moved by our confession of our nationality, owned to three "nevvies" in New Haven. So small is the world and so closely knit in the ties of a common humanity and a common citizenship, native and adoptive!

W. D. Howells

The country around York looked so beautiful from Clifford's Tower that we would not be satisfied till we had seen it closer, and we chose a bright, cool September afternoon for our drive out of the town and over the breezy, high levels which surround it. The first British capital could hardly have been more nobly placed, and one could not help grieving that the Ouse should have indolently lost York that early dignity by letting its channel fill up with silt and spoil its navigation. The Thames managed better for York's upstart rival London, and yet the Ouse is not destitute of sea or river craft. These were of both steam and sail, and I myself have witnessed the energy with which the reluctance of the indolent stream is sometimes overcome. I do not suppose that anywhere else, when the wind is low, is a vessel madly hurled through the water at a mile an hour by means of a rope tied to its mast and pulled by a fatherly old horse under the intermittent drivership of two boys whom he could hardly keep to the work. I loved the banks of a stream where one could see such a triumph of man over nature, and where nature herself was so captivating. All that grassy and shady neighborhood seemed a public promenade, where on a Sunday one could see the lower middle classes in their best and brightest, and it had for all its own the endearing and bewitching name of Ings. Why cannot we have Ings by the Hudson side?

*   *   *   *   *

TWO YORKISH EPISODES

Certainly I had not come to York, as certainly I would not have gone anywhere, for battle-fields, but becoming gradually sensible in that city that the battle of Marston Moor was fought a few miles away, and my enemy Charles I. put to one of his worst defeats there, I bought a third-class ticket and ran out to the place one day for whatever emotion awaited me there.

W. D. Howells

I

At an English station you are either overwhelmed with
transportation, or you are without any except such as you
were born with, and at the station for Marston Moor I asked
for a fly in vain. But it was a most walkable afternoon, and
the pleasant road into the region which the station-master
indicated as that I was seeking invited the foot by its level
stretch, sometimes under wayside trees, but mostly between
open fields, newly reaped and still yellow with their stubble,
or green with the rowen clover. Sometimes it ran straight and
sometimes it curved, but it led so rarely near any human
habitation that one would rather not have met any tramps
beside one's self on it. Presently I overtook one, a gentle old
farm-wife, a withered blonde, whom I helped with the
bundles she bore in either hand, in the hope that she could
tell me whether I was near Marston Moor or not. But she
could tell me only, what may have been of higher human
interest, that her husband had the grass farm of a hundred
and fifty acres, which we were coming to, for seventy-five
pounds a year; and they had their own cattle, sheep, and
horses, and were well content with themselves. She excused
herself for not knowing more than vaguely of the battle-field,
as not having been many years in the neighborhood; and
being now come to a gate in the fields, she thanked me and
took her way up a grassy path to the pleasant farmhouse I
saw in the distance.

It must have been about this time that it rained, having shone
long enough for English weather, and it hardly held up
before I was overtaken by a friendly youth on a bicycle,
whom I stayed with the question uppermost in my mind. He
promptly got off his wheel to grapple with the problem. He
was a comely young fellow, an artisan of some sort from a
neighboring town, and he knew the country well, but he did

not know where my lost battle-field was. He was sure that it was near by: but he was sure there was no monument to mark the spot. Then we parted friends, with many polite expressions, and he rode on and I walked on.

For a mile and more I met no other wayfarer, and as I felt that it was time to ask for Marston Moor again, I was very glad to be overtaken by a gentleman driving in a dog-cart, with his pretty young daughter on the wide seat with him. He halted at sight of the elderly pilgrim, and hospitably asked if he could not give him a lift, alleging that there was plenty of room. He was interested in my search, which he was not able definitely to promote, but he believed that if I would drive with him to his place I could find the battle-field, and, anyhow, I could get a trap back from the The Sun. I pleaded the heat I was in from walking, and the danger for an old fellow of taking cold in a drive through the cool air; and then, as old fellows do, we bantered each other about our ages, each claiming to be older than the other, and the kind, sweet young girl sat listening with that tolerance of youth for the triviality of age which is so charming. When he could do no more, he said he was sorry, and wished me luck, and drove on; and I being by this time tired with my three miles' tramp, took advantage of a wayside farmhouse, the first in all the distance, and went in and asked for a cup of tea.

The farm-wife, who came in out of her back garden to answer my knock, pleaded regretfully that her fire was down; but she thought I could get tea at the next house; and she was very conversable about the battle-field. She did not know just where it was, but she was sure it was quite a mile farther on; and at that I gave up the hope of it along with the tea. This is partly the reader's loss, for I have no doubt I could have been very graphic about it if I had found it; but as for Marston Moor, I feel pretty certain that if it ever existed it does not now. A moor, as I understand, implies a sort of

W. D. Howells

wildness, but nothing could be more domestic than the peaceful fields between which I had come so far, and now easily found my way back to the station. Easily, I say, but there was one point where the road forked, though I was sure it had not forked before, and I felt myself confronted with some sort, any sort, of exciting adventure. By taking myself firmly in hand, and saying, "It was yonder to the left where I met my kind bicycler, and we vainly communed of my evanescent battle-field," and so keeping on, I got safely to the station with nothing more romantic in my experience than a thrilling apprehension.

II

I quite forgot Marston Moor in my self-gratulation and my recognition of the civility from every one which had so ineffectively abetted my search. Simple and gentle, how hospitable they had all been to my vain inquiry, and how delicately they had forborne to visit the stranger with the irony of the average American who is asked anything, especially anything he does not know! I went thinking that the difference was a difference between human nature long mellowed to its conditions, and human nature rasped on its edges and fretted by novel circumstances to a provisional harshness. I chose to fancy that unhuman nature sympathized with the English mood; in the sheep bleating from the pastures I heard the note of Wordsworth's verse; and by the sky, hung in its low blue with rough, dusky clouds, I was canopied as with a canvas of Constable's.

It was the more pity, then, that at the station a shooting party, approaching from the other quarter with their servants and guns and dogs, and their bags of hares and partridges, should have given English life another complexion to the wanderer so willing to see it always rose color. The gunners gained the station platform first, and at once occupied the benches, strewing all the vacant places with their still bleeding prey. I did not fail of the opportunity to see in them the arrogance of class, which I had hitherto so vainly expected, and I disabled their looks by finding them as rude as their behavior. How different they were from the kind bicycler, or the gentleman in the dog-cart, or either one of the farm-wives who sorrowed so civilly not to know where my lost battle-field was!

In England, it is always open to the passenger to enforce a claim to his share of the public facilities, but I chose to go into the licensed victualler's next the station and sit down to a peaceable cup of tea rather than contest a place on that bloody benching; and so I made the acquaintance of an interior out of literature, such as my beloved Thomas Hardy likes to paint. On a high-backed rectangular settle rising against the wall, and almost meeting in front of the comfortable range, sat a company of rustics, stuffing themselves with cold meat, washed down with mugs of ale, and cozily talking. They gained indefinitely in my interest from being served by a lame woman, with a rhythmical limp, and I hope it was not for my demerit that I was served apart in the chillier parlor, when I should have liked so much to stay and listen to the rustic tale or talk. The parlor was very depressingly papered, but on its walls I had the exalted company of his Majesty the King, their Royal Highnesses the Prince and Princess of Wales, the late Premier, the Marquis of Salisbury, and, for no assignable reason except a general fitness for high society, the twelve Apostles in Da Vinci's *Last Supper*, together with an appropriate view of York Minster.

III

I do not pretend this search for the battle-field of Marston Moor was the most exciting episode of my stay in York. In fact, I think it was much surpassed in a climax of dramatic poignancy incident to our excursion to Bishopsthorpe, down the Ouse, on one of the cosey little steamers which ply the stream without unreasonably crowding it against its banks. It was a most silvery September afternoon when we started from the quay at York, and after escaping from embarkment on a boat going in the wrong direction, began, with no unseemly swiftness, to scuttle down the current. It was a perfect voyage, as perfect as any I ever made on the Mississippi, the Ohio, the St. Lawrence, or the Hudson, on steamers in whose cabins our little boat would have lost itself. We had a full but not crowded company of passengers, overflowing into a skiff at our stern, in which a father and mother, with three women friends, preferred the high excitement of being towed to Bishopsthorpe, where it seemed that the man of the party knew the gardener. With each curve of the river and with each remove we got the city in more and more charming retrospective, till presently its roofs and walls and spires and towers were lost in the distance, and we were left to the sylvan or pastoral loveliness of the low shores. Here and there at a pleasant interval from the river a villa rose against a background of rounded tree tops, with Lombardy poplars picking themselves out before it, but for the most part the tops of the banks, with which we stood even on our deck, retreated from the waterside willows in levels of meadow-land, where white and red cows were grazing, and now and then young horses romping away from groups of their elders. It was all dear and kind and sweet, with a sort of mid-Western look in its softness (as the English landscape often has), and the mud-banks were like those of my native Ohio Valley rivers. The effect was heightened, on our return, by an aged and virtuously poor (to all appearance) flageolet and cornet band, playing *'Way down upon the Suwanee River*, while the light played in "ditties no-tone" over the groves and pastures of the shore, and the shadows stretched themselves luxuriously out as if for a long night's sleep. There has seldom been such a day since I began to grow old; a soft September gale ruffled and tossed the trees finely, and a subtle Italian quality mixed with the American richness of the sunshiny air; so that I thought we reached Bishopsthorpe only too soon, and I woke from a pleasant reverie to be told that the steamer could not land with us, but we must be taken ashore in the small boat which we saw putting out for us from its moorings. To this day I do not know why the steamer could not land, but perhaps the small boat had a prescriptive right in the matter. At any rate, it was vigorously manned by a woman, who took tuppence from each of us for her service, and presently earned it by the interest she showed in our getting to the Archbishop's palace, or villa, the right way.

So we went round by an alluring road to its forking, where, looking up to the left, we could see a pretty village behind Lombardy poplars, and coming down toward us in a victoria for their afternoon drive, two charmingly dressed ladies, with bright parasols, and looking very county-family, as we poor Americans imagine such things out of English fiction. We entered the archiepiscopal grounds through a sympathetic Gothic screen, as I will call the overture to the Gothic edifice in my defect of architectural terminology, though perhaps gateway would be simpler; and found ourselves in the garden, and in the company of those people we had towed down behind our steamer. They were with their friend, the gardener, and, claiming their acquaintance as fellow-passengers, we made favor with him to see the house. The housekeeper, or some understudy of hers, who received us, said the family were away, but she let us follow her through.

That is more than I will let the reader do, for I know the duty of the cultivated American to the intimacies of the gentle English life; it is only with the simple life that I ever make free; there, I own, I have no scruple. But I will say (with my back turned conscientiously to the interior) that nothing could be lovelier than the outlook from the dining-room, and the whole waterfront of the house, on the wavy and willowy Ouse, and that I would willingly be many times an archbishop to have that prospect at all my meals.

W. D. Howells

IV

We despatched our visit so promptly that we got back to our boat- woman's cottage a full hour before our steamer was to call for us. She had an afternoon fire kindled in her bright range, from the oven of which came already the odor of agreeable baking. Upon this hint we acted, and asked if tea were possible. It was, and jam sandwiches as well, or if we preferred buttered tea-cake, with or without currants, to jam sandwiches, there would be that presently. We preferred both, and we sat down in that pleasant parlor-kitchen, and listened, till the tea-cake came out of the oven and was split open and buttered smoking hot, to a flow of delightful and instructive talk. For our refection we paid sixpence each, but for our edification we are still, and hope ever to be, in debt. Our hostess was of a most cheerful philosophy, such as could not be bought of most modern philosophers for money. The flour for our tea-cakes, she said, was a shilling fivepence a stone, "And not too much for growing and grinding it, and all." Every week-day morning she rose at half-past four, and got breakfast for her boys, who then rode their bicycles, or, in the snow, walked, all the miles of our voyage into York, where they worked in the railway shops. No, they did not belong to any union; the railway men did not seem to care for it; only a "benefit union."

She kept the house for her family, and herself ready to answer every hail from the steamer; but in her mellow English content, which was not stupid or sodden, but clever and wise, it was as if it were she, rather than the archbishop, whose nature expressed itself in a motto on one of the palace walls, "Blessed be the Lord who loadeth us with blessings every day."

When the range, warming to its work, had made her

kitchen-parlor a little too hot to hold us, she hospitably suggested the river shore as cooler, where she knew a comfortable log we could sit on. Thither she presently followed when the steamer's whistle sounded, and held her boat for us to get safely in. The most nervous of our party offered the reflection, as she sculled us out into the stream to overhaul the pausing steamer, that she must find the ferry business very shattering to the nerves, and she said,

"Yes, but it's nothing to a murder case I was on, once."

"Oh, what murder, what murder?" we palpitated back; and both of us forgot the steamer, so that it almost ran us down, while our ferrywoman began again:

"A man shot a nurse—There! Throw that line, will you?"

But he, who ought to have thrown the line for her, in his distraction let her drop her oar and throw the line herself, and then we scrambled aboard without hearing any more of the murder.

This is the climax I have been working up to, and I call it a fine one; as good as a story to be continued ever ended an instalment with.

*   *   *   *   *

W. D. Howells

A DAY AT DONCASTER AND
AN HOUR OUT OF DURHAM

The Doncaster Races lured us from our hotel at York, on the first day, as I had dimly foreboded they would. In fact, if there had been no lure, I might have gone in search of temptation, for in a world where sins are apt to be ugly, a horse-race is so beautiful that if one loves beauty he can practise an aesthetic virtue by sinning in that sort. So I made myself a pretence of profit as well as pleasure, and in going to Doncaster I feigned the wish chiefly to compare its high event with that of Saratoga. I had no association with the place save horse-racing, and having missed Ascot and Derby Day, I took my final chance in pursuit of knowledge—I said to myself, "Not mere amusement"—and set out for Doncaster unburdened by the lightest fact concerning the place.

I

I learned nothing of it when there, but I have since learned, from divers trustworthy sources, that Doncaster is the Danum of Antoninus and the Dona Ceaster of the Saxons, and that it is not only on the line of the Northeastern Railway, but also on that famous Watling Street which from the earliest Saxon time has crossed the British continent from sea to sea, and seems to impress most of the cities north and south into a conformity with its line, like a map of the straightest American railway routes.

Unless my ignorance has been abused, nothing remarkable has happened at Doncaster in two thousand years, but this is itself a distinction in that eventful England where so many things have happened elsewhere. It is the market town of a rich farming region, and has notable manufactures of iron and brass, of sacking and linen, of spun flax and of agricultural machines and implements. Otherwise, it is important only for its races, which began there three hundred years ago, and especially for its St. Leger Day, of which Lieutenant-General St. Leger became the patron saint in 1778, though he really established his Day two years earlier.

Doncaster is a mighty pleasant, friendly, rather modern, and commonplacely American-looking town, with two-story trams gently ambling up and down its chief avenues, in the leisurely English fashion, and all of more or less arrival and departure at the race-grounds. In our company the reader will have our appetites for lunch, and if he will take his chance with us in the first simple place away from the station, he will help us satisfy them very wholesomely and agreeably at boards which seem festively set up for the occasion, and spread with hot roast-beef and the plain vegetables which accompany the national dish in its native land; or he can have the beef cold, or have cold lamb or chicken cold. His fellow-lunchers will be, as he may like well enough to fancy, of somewhat lower degree than himself, but they will all seem very respectable, and when they come out together, they will all be equalized in the sudden excitement which has possessed itself of the street, and lined the curbstones up and down with spectators, their bodies bent forward, and their faces turned in the direction of the station.

II

The excitement is caused by the coming of the King; and I wish that I could present that event in just its sincere unimpressiveness. I have assisted at several such events on the Continent, where, especially in Germany, they are heralded as they are in the theatre, with a blare of trumpets, and a sensation in the populace and the attendant military little short of an ague fit. There, as soon as the majesties mount into their carriages from the station, they drive off as swiftly as their horses can trot, and their subjects, who have been waiting for hours to see them, make what they can of a meagre half-minute's glimpse of them. But how different was the behavior of that easy- going Majesty of England! As soon as I heard that he was coming, I perceived how anxious I had been in the half-year of my English sojourn to see him, and how bitterly I should have been disappointed to leave his realms without it. All kings are bad, I knew that well enough; but I also knew that some kings are not so bad as others, and I had been willing to accept at their face the golden opinions of this King, which, almost without exception, his lieges seemed to hold. Of course it is not hard to think well of a king if you are under him, just as it is not hard to think ill of him if you are not under him; but there is no use being bigotedly republican when there is nothing to be got by it, and I own the fact that his subjects like him willingly. Probably no man in his kingdom understands better than Edward VII. that he is largely a form, and that the more a form he is the more conformable he is to the English ideal of a monarch. But no Englishman apparently knows better than he when to leave off being a form and become a man, and he has endeared himself to his people from time to time by such inspirations. He is reputed on all hands to be a man of great good sense; if he is ever fooled it is not by himself, but by the system which he is no more a part of than the least

W. D. Howells

of his subjects. If he will let a weary old man or a delicate woman stand indefinitely before him, he is no more to blame for that than for speaking English with a trace of German in his *th* sounds; he did not invent his origins or his traditions. Personally, having had it out with life, he is as amiable and as unceremonious as a king may be. He shares, as far as he can, the great and little interests of his people. He has not, so far as noted, the gifts of some of his sisters, but he has much of his mother's steadfast wisdom, and his father's instinct for the right side in considerable questions; and he has his father's prescience of the psychological moment for not bothering. Of course, he is a fetish; no Englishman can deny that the kingship is an idolatry; but he is a fetish with an uncommon share of the common man's divinity. The system which provides him for the people provides them the best administration in the world, always naturally in the hands of their superiors, social and political; but we could be several times rottener than we administratively are, and still be incalculably reasonabler, as republicans, than those well-governed monarchists.

Some of us are apt to forget the immense advantage which we have of the monarchical peoples in having cast away the very name of King, for with the name goes the nature of royalty and all that is under and around it. But because we are largely a fond and silly folk, with a false conceit of ourselves and others, we like to make up romances about the favor in which thrones, municipalities, and powers hold us. Once it was the Tsar of Russia who held us dear, and would do almost anything for Americans; now it is the King of England who is supposed rather to prefer us to his own people, and to delight to honor us. We attribute to him a feeling which a little thought would teach, us was wholly our own, and which would be out of nature if not out of reason with him. He is a man of sense, and not of sentiment, and except as a wise politician he could have no affection for a nation whose existence denies him. He is very civil to Americans; it is part of a constitutional king's business to be civil to every one; but he is probably not sentimental about us; and we need not be sentimental about him.

He looked like a man of sense, and not like a man of sentiment, that day as he drove through the Doncaster street on his way to the sport he loves beyond any other sport. He sat with three other gentlemen on the sidewise seats of the trap, preceded by outriders, which formed the simple turnout of the greatest prince in the world. He was at the end on the right, and he showed fully as stout as he was, in the gray suit he wore, while he lifted his gray top-hat now and then, bowing casually, almost absently, to the spectators fringing, not too deeply, the sidewalks. He was very, very stout, even after many seasons of Marienbad, and after the sufferings he had lately undergone, and he was quite like the pictures and effigies of him, down to those on the postage-stamps. He has a handsome face, still bearded in the midst of a mostly clean-shaving nation, and with the white hairs prevalent on the cheeks and temples; his head is bald atop, though hardly from the uneasiness of wearing a crown.

It was difficult to realize him for what he was, and in the unmilitary keeping of a few policemen, he was not of the high histrionic presence that those German majesties were. The good- natured crowd did not strain itself in cheering, though it seemed to cheer cordially; and it did not stay long after the trap tooled comfortably away. I then addressed myself to a little knot of railway servants who lingered talking, and asked them what some carriages were still waiting for at the door of the station, and one of them answered with a lightness you do not expect in England, "Oh, Lord This, and Lady That, and the Hon. Mr. I-don't-

W. D. Howells

know-what's-his-name." The others laughed at this ribald satire of the upper classes, and I thought it safer to follow the King to the races lest I should hear worse things of them.

III

The races were some miles away, and when we got to the tracks we did not find their keeping very different from that of the Saratoga tracks, although the crowd was both smarter and shabbier, and it had got to the place through a town of tents and sheds, and a population of hucksters and peddlers, giving an effect of permanency to the festivity such as a solemnity of ours seldom has. When we bought our tickets we found, in the familiarity with the event expected of us, that there was no one to show us to our places; but by dint of asking we got to the Grand Stand, and mounted to our seats, which, when we stood up from them, commanded a wholly satisfactory prospect of the whole field.

I do not know the dimensions of the Doncaster track, or how far they exceed those of the Saratoga track. Possibly one does not do its extent justice because there is no track at Doncaster: there is nothing but a green turf, with a certain course railed off on it. I hope the reader will be as much surprised as I was to realize that the sport of horse-racing in England gets its name of Turf from the fact that the races are run on the grass, and not on the bare ground, as with us. We call the sport the Turf, too, but that is because in this, as in so many other things, we lack incentive and invention, and are fondly colonial and imitative; we ought to call it the Dirt, for that is what it is with us. As a spectacle, the racing lacks the definition in England which our course gives, and when it began, I missed the relief into which our track throws the bird-like sweep of the horses as they skim the naked earth in the distance.

I missed also the superfluity of jockeying which delays and enhances the thrill of the start with us, and I thought the English were not so scrupulous about an even start as we are.

But, above all, I missed the shining faces and the gleaming eyes of the black jockeys, who lend so much gayety to our scene, where they seem born to it, if not of it. The crowd thickened in English bloom and bulk, which is always fine to see, and bubbled over with the babble of multitudinous voices, crossed with the shouts of the book-makers. Having failed to enter any bets with the book-makers of The Pavement in York, I did not care to make them here. With all my passion for racing, I never know or care which horse wins; but I tried to enter into the joy of a diffident young fellow near me at the Grand Stand rail, who was so proud of having guessed as winner the horse next to the winner at the first race; it was coming pretty close. By the end of the third or how far they exceed those of the Saratoga track. Possibly one does not do its extent justice because there is no track at Doncaster: there is nothing but a green turf, with a certain course railed off on it. I hope the reader will be as much surprised as I was to realize that the sport of horse-racing in England gets its name of Turf from the fact that the races are run on the grass, and not on the bare ground, as with us. We call the sport the Turf, too, but that is because in this, as in so many other things, we lack incentive and invention, and are fondly colonial and imitative; we ought to call it the Dirt, for that is what it is with us. As a spectacle, the racing lacks the definition in England which our course gives, and when it began, I missed the relief into which our track throws the bird-like sweep of the horses as they skim the naked earth in the distance.

I missed also the superfluity of jockeying which delays and enhances the thrill of the start with us, and I thought the English were not so scrupulous about an even start as we are. But, above all, I missed the shining faces and the gleaming eyes of the black jockeys, who lend so much gayety to our scene, where they seem born to it, if not of it. The crowd thickened in English bloom and bulk, which is always fine to see, and bubbled over with the babble of multitudinous voices, crossed with the shouts of the book-makers. Having failed to enter any bets with the book-makers of The Pavement in York, I did not care to make them here. With all my passion for racing, I never know or care which horse wins; but I tried to enter into the joy of a diffident young fellow near me at the Grand Stand rail, who was so proud of having guessed as winner the horse next to the winner at the first race; it was coming pretty close. By the end of the third race he had softened into something like confidence toward me; certainly into conversability; such was the effect of my being a dead-game sport, or looking it. But how account for the trustfulness of the young woman on my other hand who wore her gold watch outside her dress, and who turned to the elderly stranger for sympathy in a certain supreme moment? This was when the crowd below crumpled suddenly together like the crushing of paper and the sense of something tragically mysterious in the distance clarified itself as the death of one of the horses. It had dropped from heart-break in its tracks, as if shot, and presently a string of young men and boys came dragging to some *spoliarium* the long, slender body of the pretty creature over the turf which its hoofs had beaten a moment before. Then it was that the girl, with the watch on her breast, turned and asked, "Isn't it sad?"

W. D. Howells

IV

She was probably not the daughter of a hundred earls, but there must have been some such far-descended fair among the ladies who showed themselves from time to time in the royal paddock across a little space from our Grand Stand. The enclosure has no doubt a more technical name, which I would call it by if I knew it, for I do not wish to be irreverent; but paddock is very sporty, and it must serve my occasion. The King never showed himself there at all, though much craned round for and eagerly expected. But ladies and gentlemen moved about in the close, and stood and talked together; very tall people, very easily straight and well set up, very handsome, and very amiable-looking; they may have been really kind and good, or they may have looked so to please the King and keep his spirits up. I did not then, but I do now, realize that these were courtiers, such as one has always read of, and were of very historical quality in their attendance on the monarch. I trust it will not take from the dignity of the fact if I note that several of the courtiers wore derby hats, and one was in a sack coat and a topper. I am not sure what the fairer reader will think if I tell that one of the ladies had on a dress with a white body and crimson skirt and sleeves, and a vast black picture-hat, and wore it with a charming air of authority.

The weather, in the excitement of the races, had not known whether it was raining or not, but we feared its absent-mindedness, and at the end of the third race we went away. It is not well to trust an English day too far; this had begun with brilliant sunshine, but it dimmed as it wore on, and we could not know that it was keeping for us the surprise of a very refined sunset. My memory does not serve as to just how we had got out to the race-ground; I think, from our being set down at the very gate, that it was by hansom or by fly; but now we promised ourselves to walk back to town. We did not actually do so; we went back most of the way by tram; but we were the firmer about walking at the outset, because we presently found ourselves in a lane of gypsy tents, where there was an alluring sight and smell of frying fish and potatoes. In the midst of the refection, you could have your fortune told, very favorably, for a very little money. All up and down this happy avenue there went girls of several dozen sizes and ages, crying a particular kind of taffy, proper to the day and place, and never to be had on any other day in any other place.

We had an hour before train-time, and we thought we would go and see the Parish Church of Doncaster, which we had read was worth seeing. Our belief was confirmed by a group of disappointed ladies in the churchyard, who said it was a most beautiful church inside, but that they had not seen it because it was shut. We proved the fact by trying the door, and then we came away consoling ourselves with the scoff that it was probably closed for the races. At the bookseller's, where we stopped to buy some photographs of the interior of the church we had not seen, we lamented our disappointment, and the salesman said, "Perhaps it was closed for the races." So our joke seemed to turn earnest, and on reflection it did not surprise us in that England of close-knit unities where people and prince are of one texture in their pleasures and devotions, and the Church is hardly more national than the Turf.

W. D. Howells

V

At Durham, which was my next excursion from York, I cannot claim, therefore, that my mission was more serious because it almost solely concerned the Church, or that it was more frivolous at Doncaster, where it almost solely concerned the Turf. My train started in a fine mist that turned to sun, but not before it had shown me with the local color, which a gray light lends everything, a pack of hounds crossing a field near the track with two huntsmen at their heels. They were not chasing, but running leisurely, and with their flower-like, loose spread over the green, and the pink-coated hunters on their brown mounts, they afforded a picture as vivid and of as perfect semblance to all my visions of fox-hunting as I could have asked. I had been hoping that I might see something of the famous sport, almost as English as the Church or the Turf, and there, suddenly and all unexpectedly, the sight fully and satisfyingly was. Now, indeed, I felt that my impression of English society was complete, and that I might go home and write novels of English high life, and do something to redeem myself a little from the disgrace I had fallen into with my fellow-plebeians by always writing of common Americans, like themselves, and never *grandes dames* or ideal persons, or people in the best society.

But I did not want to go home at once, or turn back from going to Durham through that pleasant landscape, where the mist hung between the trees which seemed themselves only heavier bulks of mist. The wheat in some of the fields was still uncut, and in others, where it had been gathered into sheaves, the rooks by hundreds were noisily gleaning in the track of the reapers. From this conventionally English keeping, I passed suddenly to the sight of the gaunt, dry, gravelly bed of a wide river, such as I had known in Central Italy, or the Middle West at home; and I realized once again that England is no island of one simple complexion, but is a condensed continent, with all continental varieties of feature in it. You must cover thousands and thousands of miles in our tedious lengths and breadths for the beauties and sublimities of scenery which you shall gather from fewer hundreds in England; I have no doubt they have even volcanoes there, but I did not see any, probably because the English are so reticent, and hate to make a display of any sort.

W. D. Howells

VI

It is because they are so, or possibly because of my ignorance, that I did not know or at all imagine how magnificent
the Cathedral of Durham is, or what a matchless seat it has
on the bluffs of the river, with depths of woods below its
front, tossing in the rich chill of the September wind. As it
takes flight for the heavens, to which its business is to invite
the thought, it seems to carry the earth with it, for if you
climb those noble heights, you find your feet still on the
ground, in a most stately space of open level between the
cathedral and its neighbor castle, which alone could be
worthy of its high company.

The castle is Tudor, but the cathedral is beyond all other
English cathedrals, I believe, Norman, though to the naked
eye it looks so Gothic, and probably is. Here I will leave the
reader with any pictures or memories of it which he happens
to have, for I have always held it a sin to try describing
architecture, or if not a sin, a bore. What chiefly remains to
me of my impression of Durham Cathedral is, strangely
enough, an objection: I did not like those decorated pillars,
alternating with the clustered columns of the interior, and I
do not suppose I ever shall: the spiral furrows, the zigzag and
lozenge figures chiselled in their surfaces, weakened them to
the eye and seemed to trifle with their proud bulk.

But to the castle of Durham I have no objection whatever. I
should like to live in it, as I should in all other Tudor houses,
great or small, that I saw, where, as I am constantly saying, a
high ideal of comfort is realized. It is almost as nobly placed
as the cathedral, and it is approached by a very stately court-
yard, of like spacious effect with the cathedral piazza. Inside
it there is a kitchen of the sixteenth century, with a company
of neat serving-maids, too comely and young to be, perhaps,

of the same period, that gives the tourist a high sense of the luxury in which the Bishop of Durham and the Judges of the Assize Courts live when they are residents in the castle. One sees their apartments, dim and rich, and darkly furnished, but not gloomily, both where they sleep and where they eat, and flatteringly envies them in a willingness for the moment to be a judge or a bishop for the sake of such a fit setting. There is also a fine crypt, with a fine dining-hall and a black staircase of ancient oak, and a gallery with classic busts, and other pictures worthy of wonder, let alone a history from the time of William the Conqueror, who first fancied a castle where it stands, down to the present day. The memory of such successive guests as the Empress Matilda and Henry II. her son, King John, Henry III., Edwards I., II., and III., Queen Philippa, Henry VI., and James I., and Charles I., and Edward VII., abides in the guidebook, and may be summoned from its page to the chambers of the beautiful old place by any traveller intending impressions for literary use from a medieval environment in perfect repair.

W. D. Howells

VII

One must be hard to satisfy if one is not satisfied with
Durham Castle, and its interior contented me as fully as the
exterior of the Cathedral. I went a walk, after leaving the
castle, for a further feast of the Cathedral from the paths
along the shelving banks of the beautiful Weare. There, at a
certain point, I met a studious-looking gentleman who I am
sure must have been a professor of Durham University hard
by; and I asked him, with due entreaty for pardon, "What
river was that." He quelled the surprise he must have felt at
my ignorance and answered gently, "The Weare." "Ah, to be
sure! The Weare," I said, and thanked him, and longed for
more talk with him, but felt myself so unworthy that I had
not the face to prompt him further. He passed, and then I met
a man much more of my own kind, if not probably so little
informed. That rich, chill gale was still tossing and buffeting
the tree tops, and he made occasion of this to say, "This is a
cold wynd a-blowin', Mister." "It is, rather," I assented. "I
was think-in'," he observed from an apparent generalization,
"that I wished I was at home." Then he suddenly added,
"Help a poor man!" I was not wholly surprised at the climax,
and I offered him, provisionally, a penny. "Will that do?" He
hesitated perceptibly; then he allowed, with a subtle reluctance, "Yes, that'll do," and so passed on to satisfy, I hope,
the wish he thought he had.

I pursued my own course, as far as the bridge which spans
the Weare near a most picturesque mill, and then I stopped a
kindly- looking workman and asked him whether he thought
I could find a fly or cab anywhere near that would take me
into the town. He answered, briefly but consistently with his
looks, "Ah doot," and as he owned that it was a long way to
town, I let his doubt decide me to go back to the station.

I felt that I ought to have driven from there into the town, and seen it, and taken to York a later train than the one I had in mind. In the depravity induced by my neglect of this plain duty, I went, with my third class return ticket conscious in my pocket, into the first class refreshment room, and had tea there, as if I had been gentry at the very least, and possibly nobility. Then, having a good deal of time still on my hands, I loitered over the book-stall of the station, and stole a passage of conversation with a kindly clergyman whom I found looking at the pretty shilling editions filling the cases. I said, How nice it was to have Hazlitt in that green cloth; and he said, Yes, but he held for Gibbon in leather; and just then his train came in and he ran off to it, and left me to my guilt in not having gone to see Durham. It was now twilight, and too late; but there the charming old town still is, and will long remain, I hope, with its many memories of war and peace, for whoever will visit it. Certainly there had been no lack of adventures in my ample hour. It was as charming to weave my conjectures, about the two gentlemen with whom I had so barely spoken, as to have carried my acquaintance with them further, and I cannot see how it would have profited me to know more even of that fellow-man who, in the cold wynd a- blowing, had just been thinking he wished he was at home.

* * * * *

W. D. Howells

THE MOTHER OF THE AMERICAN ATHENS

It was fit that on our way to Boston we should pause in passing through Cambridge. That was quite as we should have done at home, and I can only wish now that we had paused longer, though every moment that kept us from Boston, if it had been anywhere but in England, would have been a loss. There, it was all gain, and all joy, the gay September 24th that we went this divine journey. My companion was that companionable archaeologist who had guided my steps in search of the American origins in London, and who was now to help me follow the Pilgrim Fathers over the ground where they sojourned when they were only the Pilgrim Sons. At divers places on the way, after we left London, he pointed out some scene associated with American saints or heroes. We traversed the region that George William Curtis' people came from, hard by Roxburgh, and Eliot's, the Apostle to the Indians; again we skirted the Ralph Waldo Emerson country, with its big market town of Bishop's Stortford; and beyond Ely, where we stopped for the Cathedral and a luncheon, not unworthy of it, at the station, he startled me from a pleasant drowse I had fallen into in our railway carriage, with the cry: "There! That is where Captain John Smith was born." "Where? Where?" I implored too late, looking round the compartment everywhere. "Back where those chickens were."

I

That was the nearest I came to seeing one of the most famous Virginian origins. But you cannot see everything in England; there are too many things; and if the truth must be known I cared more for the natural features than the historical facts of the landscape. The country was flat, and a raw green, as it should be in that raw air, under that dun sky, with sheep hardily biting the short tough pasturage under the imbrowning oaks and elms, and the olive-graying willows, beside the full, still streams scarce wetter than the ground they dreamed through.

We did not reach Boston until six o'clock, when the day was already waning, and the Stump of St. Botolph's Church stood dim against the sky. It was a long drive through the suburban streets from the station to the hotel, which we found full, and which with its crazy floors touched the fancy as full of something besides guests. But it was well for us so, because across the market-place, which forms the chief public square of Boston, was a far better hotel, where we were welcomed to the old-fashioned ideal of the English inn, such as I did not so nearly realize anywhere else. The ideal was a little impaired by the electric light in our bedrooms, but it was not a very brilliant electric light, and there was a damp cold in the corridors which allowed no doubt of its genuineness. In the dining-room, which was also the reading-room, there was an admirable image of a fire in the grate, and a prevailing warmth and brightness which cheered the heart of exile. When we presently had dinner, specialized for us by certain differences from that of two other travellers, there seemed nothing more to ask, except the conversation of our companions, and this we duly had, quite as if we were four wayfarers met there in a book. One of these gentlemen proved a solicitor from Bath, and that made me feel more at home, knowing and loving Bath as I did. It did not matter that in trying for some mutual acquaintance there we failed; our good-will was everything; and the solicitor was intelligent and agreeable. The other gentleman, tall, dark, of urbane stateliness, was something more, in the touch of Oriental suavity which, more than his nose, betrayed him; and it appeared, in delightful suggestion of the old-time commercial intimacy of the Dutch and English coasts, that he was from Holland, and next morning at breakfast he developed a large valise, which I now think held samples. If he was a Dutch Jew, he was probably a Spanish Jew by descent, and what will the difficult reader have more, in the materials for his romance? Did we gather about the grate after we had done dinner, and each tell the story of his life, or at least the most remarkable thing that had ever happened to him?

I cannot say, but I remember that my friend and I, in my instant hunger for Boston, which was greater than my hunger for dinner, set forth while the meal was preparing, and visited the Church of St. Botolph. To reach it we had to pass through the greater length of the market-place, one of the most picturesque in England, and the worthy ancestress of Faneuil Hall and Quincy market-places, which are the most picturesque in America. At one side of its triangle is the birthplace and dwelling of Jean Ingelow, and at the point nearest the church is the statue of Herbert Ingram, the less famous but more locally recognized Bostonian, who founded the *Illustrated London News* with the money he made by the invention and sale of Old Parr's Pills. He was thrice sent to Parliament from his native town, and he related it to America, after two centuries, by drowning in Lake Michigan. "R. N.," the otherwise anonymous author of a very intelligent and agreeable *Handbook of Boston*, relates that in his first canvass for Parliament Ingram was opposed by a gentleman who, when he asked the voices of the voters, after the old

English fashion, was told by four of them in succession that they were promised "to their cousin Ingram," and who thereupon declared that if he had known Ingram "was cousin to the whole town" he would, never have stood against him. Like the Bostonians of Massachusetts, the Bostonians of Lincolnshire were in fact closely knit together by ties of kinship, owing, "R. N." believes, to the isolation of Boston before the draining of its fens, and not to their conviction that there were no outsiders worthy to mate with them.

W. D. Howells

II

The house where the martyrologist John Fox first saw the light was replaced long ago by a famous old inn, pulled down in its turn; but the many and many Americans who visit Boston may still visit the house where Jean Ingelow was born. Whether they may see more than the outside of it I do not know from experiment or even inquiry. "R. N." will say nothing of her but that she was born, and that her father was a banker; perhaps he thinks that she has spoken sufficiently for herself.

The air of the market-place, as we crossed to the church, was of a pleasant bleakness, and the Witham was coldly washing under the wall which keeps St. Botolph from it. In the dimness we could have only a conjecture of the church's outward beauty, and of the grandeur of the tower climbing into the evening, where it has hailed so many myriads of moving ships, and beckoned them to safety. But within, where it was already night, the church was cheerfully luminous with Welsbach lights, which showed it all wreathed and garlanded for a harvest festival, began the day before, and to be concluded now with some fit religious observance. The blossoms and leaves were a little wilted and withered, but the fruits and vegetables were there in sturdy endurance, and together they swathed the pulpit from which John Cotton used to preach, and all but hid its structure from view, like flowers of rhetoric softening some hard doctrine.

Apparently, however, Cotton's doctrine was not anywise too hard, or even hard enough, for such "a factious people, who were imbued with the Puritan spirit," as he found in Boston, when he was first elected vicar of St. Botolph's; and it was not till Archbishop Laud's ecclesiastical tyrannies began that he came to see "the Sin of Conformity" and to preach resistance. His conflict with the authorities went so far that exile to another Boston in another hemisphere became his only hope. Or, as Lord Dorset intimated, "if he had been guilty of drunkenness, uncleanness, or any lesser fault, he could have obtained his pardon, but as he was guilty of Puritanism, and Non-conformity, the crime was non-pardonable; and therefore he advised him to flee for his safety."

The Cotton Chapel, so called, was restored mainly with moneys received from Cotton's posterity, lineal or lateral, in his city of refuge overseas, and "the corbels that support the timbered ceiling are carved with the arms of certain of the early colonists of New England." Edward Everett, one of Cotton's descendants, wrote the dedicatory inscription in Latin, which "R. N." has Englished in verse, and I am the more scrupulous to quote it, because, as I must own with my usual reluctant honesty, I quite missed seeing the Cotton Chapel.

That here John Cotton's memory may survive
Where for so long he labored when alive,
In James' reign and Charles', ere it ceased—
A grave, skilled, learned, earnest parish-priest;
Till from the strife that tossed the Church of God
He in a new world sought a new abode,
To a new England, a new Boston came,
(That took, to honor him, that reverend name)
Fed the first flock of Christ that gathered there—
Till death deprived it of its shepherd's care—
There well resolved all doubts of mind perplext,
Whether with cares of this world or the next;
Two centuries five lustra from the year
That saw the exile leave his labors here,
His family, his townsmen, with delight—
(Whom to the task their English kin invite)—

To the fair fane he served so well of yore,
His name, in two worlds honored, thus restore,
This chapel renovate, this tablet place,
In this, the year of man's recovered Grace,
1855.

III

I missed most of the other memorable things in the church that night, but I saw fleetingly some of the beautiful tombs for which it is famous; the effigies of the dead lay in their niches, quietly, as if already tucked away for the night, in the secular sleep of the dust beneath. The tombs were more famous than they, and more beautiful, if the faces of some were true likenesses, but after so many centuries one ought not to require even women to be pretty.

We had not begun to have enough of Boston yet, and after dinner we went a long walk up the Witham, away from the parapet before the church, under which its deep tides are always washing to and fro. In the dimness, after we had got a little to the outskirts of the town, there seemed shipyards along the river's course, but at one place there was a large building brilliantly lighted, which from certain effects at the windows we decided to be a printing-office on the scale of those in and near our own Boston. What was our shame and grief the next morning to find it was a cigar factory, and to learn that cigar and cigarette making was almost the chief industry of the mother Boston. There are really two large tobacco factories there running overtime, and always advertising for more women and girls to do their work; and in our Boston, not so long ago, smoking in the street was forbidden! Such are the ironies of life.

What the shipyards had turned into by daylight, I do not now remember. The Witham had turned into a long, deep gash, cut down into the clay twenty feet from the level of the flood tides. We crossed on a penny ferry which the current pushed over in the manner of the earliest ferries, near the tobacco factory, and came back into the heart of the town through streets of low stone houses, with few buildings of note to dignify their course. Small craft lay along the steep muddy shores, and at one place a little excursion steamer was waiting for the tide to come in and float it for the fulfilment of its promise of sailing at ten o'clock. We idly longed to make its voyage with it, and if the chance were offering now, I certainly should not forego it as I did then. But when you are in a foreign place, no matter how much you have travelled and how well you know that it will not offer soon again, you reject the most smiling chance because you think you can take it any time.

The morning was soft and warm, with a sun shining amiably on the rather commonplace old town. I had risen betimes that I might go and get a Spanish melon for my breakfast, but at eight o'clock I found the fruiterer's locked and barred against me. I lingered and hungered for the melons which I saw in his window, and then I tried other fruiterers, but none of them was stirring yet. I reflected how different it would have been in our own Boston; and if it had not been for the market people coming into the square and beginning to dress their stalls with vegetables, and fish, and native fruits, such as hard pears and knotty apples, I do not know how ill I might have come away thinking of that idle mother Boston. In other squares there were cattle for sale later, and fish, but I cannot in even my present leniency claim that the markets were open at the hour which the genteeler commerce of the place found so indiscreet. They were irregular spaces of a form in keeping with the general shambling and shapeless character of the town, which, once for all, I must own was not an impressive place.

The best thing in it, and the thing you are always coming back to, is the beautiful church, to which we paid a second visit early in the forenoon. We found it where we left it the night before, lifting its tower from the brink of the Witham, and looking far out over the flat land to a sea no flatter. The land seems indeed, like so much English coast, merely the sea come ashore, and turned into fens for the greater convenience of the fishermen, whom, with the deeper sea sailors, we saw about the town, lounging through the crooked streets, and hanging bare- armed upon the parapets of the bridges. Now we found the church had about its foot a population of Bostonians for whom, under their flat gravestones, it had been chiming the quarters from its mellow-throated bells, while the Bostonians on our side had been hustling for liberty, and money, and culture, and all the good things of this world, and getting them in a measure that would astonish their namesakes. Within the church we saw again the beautiful tombs of the night before, and others like them, and again we saw the pulpit of John Cotton, which we could make out a little better than at first, because its garlands were a little more withered and shrunken away. But better than either we realized the perfection of the church interior as a whole, so ample, so simple, such a comfortable and just sufficient eyeful.

IV

From other interests in St. Botolph's you somehow keep always, or finally, coming to the Stump, as the tower is called somewhat in the humor of our Boston. It is not so fair within as without; that could not be in the nature of things; and yet the interior of the tower has a claim upon the spectator's wonder, if not his admiration, which, so far as I know, the interior of no other tower has. It is all treated as a loftier room of the church, and its ceiling, a hundred and fifty feet from the ground, is elaborately and allegorically groined. The work was done when the whole church was restored about half a century ago, and has not the claim of medieval whim upon the fancy. Not so much pleasure as he might wish mingles with the marvel of the beholder, who carries a crick in the neck away from the sight, and yet once, but not more, in a way, it is worth while to have had the sight. Certainly this treatment of the tower is unique; there is nothing to compare with it in Boston, Massachusetts, and cannot be even when the interior of the Old South is groined.

When we came out of the church, we found the weather amusing itself as usual in England, raining with wind, then blowing without rain, and presently, but by no means decisively, sunning without either wind or rain. The conditions were favorable to a further exploration of the town, which seemed to have a passion for old cannon, and for sticking them about in all sorts of odd nooks and corners. We found one smaller piece over a gateway, which we were forbidden by a sign-board to enter on pain of prosecution for trespassing. There was nothing else to prevent our entering, and we went in, to find ourselves in an alley with nothing but a Gypsy van in it. Nothing but a Gypsy van! As if that were not the potentiality of all manner of wild romance! Whether the alley belonged to Gypsies, or the Gypsies had trespassed by leaving their van in it, I shall now probably never know, but I commend the inquiry to any reader of mine whom these pages shall inspire to repeat our pilgrimage.

There was no great token of genteel life in Boston, so far as we saw it, but perhaps we did not look in the right places. There were good shops, but not fine or large ones, and I am able to report of the intellectual status that there are three weekly newspapers, but no dailies, which could not be the case in any American town of fourteen thousand people. Concerning society, I can only say that in our wanderings we came at one point on a vast, high-walled, iron-gated garden, which looked as if it might have society beyond it, but not being positively forbidden we did not penetrate it. We did indeed visit the ancient grammar-school, one of those foundations which in England were meant originally for the poor deserving of scholarship, but which have nearly all lapsed to the more deserving rich, careful of the contamination of the lower classes. Being out of term the school was closed to its pupils, but we found a contractor there removing the old stoves and putting in a system of hot-water heating, which he said was better fitted to resist the cold of the Boston winters. He was not a very conversable man, but so much we screwed out of him, with the added fact that the tuition of that school was no longer free. It came to some five guineas a year, no great sum, but perhaps sufficient to keep the school, with the other influences, select enough for the patronage to which it had fallen. It was a pleasant place, with a playground before it, which in the course of generations there must have been a good deal of schoolboy fun got out of.

W. D. Howells

V

There remained for us now only the Guildhall to visit, and we had left that to the last because it was the thing that had mostly brought us to Boston. It was the scene of the trial and imprisonment of those poor people of the region roundabout who were trying to escape from their "dread lord," James the First, and were arrested for this crime, and brought to answer for it before the magistrates of the town. Their dread lord had then lately met some ministers of their faith at Hampton Court, and there browbeaten, if not beaten, them in argument, so that he was in no humor to let, these people, who afterward became the Pilgrim Fathers, get away to Holland, where there was no dread lord, or at least none of King James' thinking.

But no words can be so good to tell of all this as the words of Governor Bradford in his *Historie of Plymouth Plantation*, where he says that "ther was a large companie of them purposed to get passage at Boston in Lincolnshire, and for that end had hired a shipe wholy to them selves, & made agreement with the maister to be ready at a certaine day, and take them and their goods in, at a conveniente place, wher they accordingly would all attende in readiness. So after long waiting, & large expences, though he kepte not day with them, yet he came at length & tooke them in, in the night. But when he had them & their goods abord, he betrayed them, haveing before hand complotted with the serchers & other officers so to doe; who tooke them, and put them into open boats, & ther rifled and ransaked them, searching them to their shirts for money, yea even the women furder then became modestie; and then caried them back into the towne, & made them a spectakle & wonder to the multitude, which came flocking on all sides to behould them. Being thus first, by the catchpoule officer, rifled, & stripte of their money, books, and much other goods, they were presented to the magistrates, and messengers sente to informe the lords of the Counsell of them; and so they were comited to ward. Indeed the magistrats used them courteously, and shewed them what favour they could; but could not deliver them till order came from the Counsell-table. But the issue was that after a months imprisonmente, the greatest parte were dismiste, & sent to the places from whence they came; but 7. of the principall were still kept in prison, and bound over to the Assises."

My excellent "R. N." of the *Handbook of Boston* is anxious to have his reader, as I in turn am anxious to have mine, distinguish between these future Pilgrim Fathers and the gentlemen and scholars who later founded Boston in Massachusetts Bay, and called its name after that of the town they had dwelt in or often visited before they left the handsome keeping of the gentler life of Lincolnshire. Such were Richard Bellingham, Edmund Quincy, Thomas Leverett, John Cotton, Samuel Whiting, and others, known to our colonial and national history. Not even Bradford or Brewster, afterward dignified figures in Plymouth colony, were of the humble band, men, women, and children, that the officers of Boston took from their vessel. "Pathetic but splendid figures," my brave "R. N." calls them, and he tells how, after a month's jail, they were "sent home broken men, to endure the scoffs of their neighbors and the rigors of ecclesiastical discipline."

VI

The dungeons which remain to witness of their hardships in Boston are of thick-walled, iron-grated stone, and the captives were fed on bread and water within smell of the roasting and broiling of the Guildhall kitchens immediately beside them. I will not conjecture with "R. N." that they were put there "by a refinement of cruelty," so that they might suffer the more in that vicinage. "The magistrates" who had "used them courteously and shewed them what favour they could," would not have willed that; but perhaps "the Counsell-table" did; and it was certainly a hardship that the dungeons and the kitchens were so close together, as any man may see at this day. Neither the dungeons nor the kitchens are any longer used; the spits and grates are rusted where the fires blazed, and the cells where the Pilgrims suffered are now full of large earthen jars. For no other or better reason, the large open spaces of the basement outside of them were scattered about with agricultural implements, ploughs, harrows, and the like. It was the belief of my companion, founded on I know not what fact, that the hall in which the Pilgrims were tried was a large upper chamber which we found occupied by a boys' school. The door stood partly ajar, and we could see the master within walking up and down before some twenty boys, as if waiting for one of them to answer some question he had put them. Perhaps it was a question of local history, for none of them seemed able to answer it; presently when a boy came out on some errand, and we stopped him, and asked him where it was the Pilgrims had been tried, he did not know, and apparently he had never heard of the Pilgrims. He was a very nice-looking boy, and otherwise not unintelligent; certainly he was well-mannered, as nice-looking English boys are apt to be with their elders; perhaps he had heard too much of the Pilgrims, and had purposely forgotten them. This might very well have happened in a place like Boston where such hordes of Americans are coming every year, and asking so many hard questions concerning an incident of local history not wholly creditable to the place. He could justly have said that the same or worse might have happened to the Pilgrims anywhere else in England, under the dread lord there then was, and in fact something of the same hardship did befall them afterward at the place a little northeast of Boston, which we were now to visit for their piteous sake.

"The nexte spring after," as Bradford continues the narrative of their sorrows, "ther was another attempte made by some of these & others, to get over at an other place. And so it fell out, that they light of a Dutchman at Hull, having a ship of his owne belonging to Zealand; they made agreements with him, and acquainted him with their condition, hoping to find more faithfullnes in him, then in the former of their owne nation. He bad them not fear, for he would doe well enough. He was by appointment to take them in betweene Grimsbe & Hull, where was a large comone a good way distante from any towne. Now against the prefixed time, the women & children, with the goods, were sent to the place in a small barke, which they had hired for that end; and the men were to meete them by land. But it so fell out, that they were ther a day before the shipe came, and the sea being rough, and the women very sicke, prevailed with the seamen to put into a creeke hardby, wher they lay on ground at lowwater. The nexte morning the shipe came, but they were fast, & could not stir till about noone. In the mean time, the shipe maister, perceiveing how the matter was, sente his boate to be getting the men abord whom he saw ready, walking aboute the shore. But after the first boat full was gott abord, & she was ready to goe for more, the Mr. espied a greate company, both horse & foote, with bills, & gunes, & other weapons; for the countrie was raised to take them. The Dutchman seeing this swore his countries oath, 'sacremente,' and having the wind faire, waiged his Ancor, hoysed sayles, & away. But the poore men which were gott abord, were in great distress for their wives and children, which they saw thus to be taken, and were left destitute of their helps; and them selves also, not having a cloath to shifte them with, more then they had on their baks, & some scarce a peney aboute them, all they had being abord the barke. It drew tears from their eyes, and any thing they had they would have given to have been a shore againe; but all in vaine, ther was no remedy, they must thus sadly part. The rest of the men there were in greatest danger, made shift to escape away before the troope could surprise them: those only staying that best might, to be assistante unto the women. But pitifull it was to see the heavie case of these poore women in this distress: what weeping & crying on every side, some for their husbands, that were carried away in the ship as is before related; others not knowing what should become of them, & their little ones; others again melted in teares, seeing their poore little ones hanging aboute them, crying for feare, and quaking with could. Being thus aprehanded, they hurried from one place to another, and from one justice to another, till in the ende they knew not what to doe with them; for to imprison so many women & innocent children for no other cause (many of them) but that they must goo with their husbands, seemed to be unreasonable and all would crie out of them; and to send them home againe was as difficult, for they aleged, as the trueth was, they had no homes to goe to, for they had either sould, or otherwise disposed of their houses & livings. To be shorte, after they had been thus turmoyled a good while, and conveyed from one constable to another, they were glad to be ridd of them in the end upon any termes: for all were wearied & tired with them. Though in the mean time they (poore soules) indured miserie enough; and thus in the end necessitie forste a way for them."

VII

If there is any more touching incident in the history of man's inhumanity to man, I do not know it, or cannot now recall it; and it was to visit the scene of it near "Grimsbe," or Great Grimsby, as it is now called, that we set out, after viewing their prison in Boston, over wide plains, with flights of windmills alighted on them everywhere. Here and there one seemed to have had its wings clipped, and we were told by a brighter young fellow than we often had for a travelling companion that this was because steam had been put into it as a motive power more constant than wind, even on that wind-swept coast. There seems to have been nothing else, so far as my note-book witnesses, to take up our thoughts in the short run to Great Grimsby, and for all I know now I may have drowsed by many chicken-yards marking the birthplace of our discoverers and founders. We got to Great Grimsby in time for a very lamentable lunch in a hostelry near the station, kept, I think, for such "poore people" as the Pilgrims were, with stomachs not easily turned by smeary marble table-tops with a smeary maid having to take their orders, and her ineffective napkin in her hand. The honesty as well as the poverty of the place was attested, when, returning to recover a forgotten umbrella, we were met at the door by this good girl, who had left her bar to fetch it in anticipation of all question.

At Great Grimsby, it seemed, there was no vehicle but a very exceptional kind of cab,—looking like a herdic turned wrongside fore, and unable to orient itself aright,—available for the long drive to that "large comone a good way distante from any towne," which we were to make, if we wished to visit the scene of the Pilgrims' sufferings in their second attempt to escape from their dread lord. In this strange equipage, therefore, we set out, and nine long miles we drove

W. D. Howells

through a country which seemed to rise with increasing surprise at us and our turnout on each inquiry we made for the way from chance passers. Just beyond the suburbs of the town we entered the region of a vast, evil smell which we verified as that of the decaying fish spread upon the fields, for a fertilizer after they had missed their market in that great fishing centre. Otherwise the landscape was much the ordinary English landscape of the flatter parts, but wilder and rougher than in the south or west, and constantly growing more so as we drove on and on. Our cabman kept a good courage, as long as the highway showed signs of much travel, but when it began to falter away into a country road, he must have lost faith in our sanity, though he kept an effect of the conventional respect for his nominal betters which English cabmen never part with except in a dispute about fares and distances. We stayed him as well as we could with some grapes and pears, which we found we did not want after our lunch, and which we handed him up through his little trap-door, but a plaintive quaver grew into his voice, and he let his horse lag in the misgiving which it probably shared with him. Nothing of signal interest occurred in our progress except at one point, near a Methodist chapel, where we caught sight of a gayly painted blue van, lettered over with many texts and mottoes, which my friend explained as one of the vans intinerantly used by extreme Protestants of the Anne Askew persuasion to prevent the spread of Romanism in England.

The signs of travel had not only ceased, but a little in front of us the way was barred by a gate, and beyond this gate there was nothing but a sort of savage pasture, with many red and brown cattle in it, gathered questioningly about the barrier, or lifting their heads indifferently from the grass. Just before we reached the gate we passed a peasant's cottage, where he was sociably getting in his winter's coal, and he and his wife and children, and the carter, all leaned upon whatever supports they found next them, and stared at the extra-ordinary apparition of two, I hope, personable strangers driving in a hansom of extreme type into a cow pasture. But we were not going to give ourselves away to their too probable ignorance by asking if that were the place where the Pilgrims who founded New England were first stopped from going to Holland.

My friend dismounted, and opened the gate, and we drove in among the cattle, and after they had satisfied a peaceful curiosity concerning us, they went about their business of eating grass, and we strayed over "the large comone," and tried to imagine its looks nearly three hundred years before. They could not have been very different; the place could hardly have been much wilder, and there was the "creeke hardby wher they lay," the hapless women and children, in their boat "at lowwater," while the evening came on, no doubt, just as it was doing with us, the weather clearing, and the sunset glassy and cold. Off yonder, away across the solitary moor, was the course of the Humber, marked for us by the trail of a steamer's smoke through the fringes of trees, and for them by the sail of the Dutchman, who, when he saw next day that "great company, both horse and foote, with bills and gunes, and other weapons," coming to harry those poor people, "swore his countries oath, 'sacremente,' and having the wind faire, waiged his ancor, hoysed sails, and away," leaving those desolate women and their little ones lamenting.

VIII

On our way back we stopped at a little country church, so peaceful, so very peaceful, in the evening light, where it stood, withdrawn from the highway, Norman and Gothic without, and within all so sweet and bare and clean, that we could not believe in the old ecclesiasticism which persecuted the Puritans into the exile whither they carried the persecuting spirit with them. A pretty child, a little girl, opened the churchyard gate and held it for us to pass, and her gentleness made me the more question the history of those dreadful days in the past. When I saw a young lady, in the modern dress which I had so often lost my heart to at the Church Parade in Hyde Park, going up a leafy lane, toward the vicarage, from having been for tennis and afternoon tea at some pleasant home in the neighborhood, I denied the atrocious facts altogether. She had such a very charming hat on.

The suburbs of Great Grimsby, after you reach them through that zone of bad smell, are rather attractive, and you get into long clean streets of small stone houses, like those of Plymouth or Southampton, and presently you reach the Humber, which is full of the steamers and sail, both fishing and deep sea, of the prosperous port, with great booms of sawlogs from Norway, half filling the channel, and with a fringe of tall chimneys from the sawmills along the shores. Great Grimsby is not only the centre of a vast distributing trade in coal and lumber, but of a still vaster trade in fish. It cuts one's pride, if one has believed that Gloucester, Massachusetts, is the greatest fishing port in the world, to learn that Grimsby, with a hundred more fishing sail, is only "*one* of the principal fishing ports" of the United Kingdom. What can one do against those brutal British statistics? We think our towns grow like weeds, but London seems to grow half such a weed as Chicago in a single night.

After we were got well into the town, we found ourselves part of an immense bicycle parade, with bicyclers of both sexes on their wheels, in masks and costumes, Pierrots, and Clowns, and Harlequins and Columbines, in a competition for the prettiest and fanciest dress.

When we came to start from the station on our run to London, we reflected that there were a great many of these bicyclers, and that they would probably crowd us in our third-class compartment. So, as we had bought an excellent supper in baskets, such as they send you on the trains everywhere in England, and wished to eat it in quiet, we sought out the guard who was lurking near for the purpose, and bribed him to shut us into that compartment, and not let any one else in. There we remained in darkness, with our curtains drawn, and when, near train-time, the bicyclers began to swarm about the carriages, we heard them demanding admittance to our compartment from our faithful guard, if that is the right way to call him. He turned them away with soft answers, answers so very soft that we could not make out what he said, but he seemed to be inviting them into other compartments, which he doubtless pretended were better. The murmurs would die away, and then rise again, and from time to time we knew that a baffled bicycler was pulling at our door, or vainly bumping against it. We listened with our hearts in our mouths; but no one got in, and the train started, and we opened our baskets and began to eat and to drink, like two aristocrats or plutocrats. What made our inhuman behavior worse was that we were really nothing of the kind, but both professed friends of the common people. The story might show that when it comes to a question of selfishness men are all alike ready to profit by the unjust conditions. However, it must be remembered that those people were only bicyclers. If we could have conceived of

W. D. Howells

them as masses we should have known them for brothers, and let them in, probably.

* * * * *

ABERYSTWYTH, A WELSH WATERING-PLACE

It is only some six or seven hours by train from London to Aberystwyth, but if you will look at the names on a map of the Cambrian railways, when you begin the Welsh part of your journey, you will seem to be in a stranger and farther country than that of Prester John. Pwllheli, Cerrig y Drudion, Gwerful Goch, Festiniog, Bryn Eglwys, Llanidloes, Maertwro, Carnedd Fibast, Clynog Fwr, Llan-y-Mawddwy Machynlleth, Duffws, are a few out of the hundred names in the hills or along the valleys, giving the near neighborhood of England an effect of more than mid-Asian remoteness. The eye starts at their look; but if the jaw aches at the thought of pronouncing them, it is our own wilful orthographical usage that is at fault; the words, whose sound the letters faithfully render, are music, and they largely record a Christian civilization which was centuries old when the Saxons came to drive the Britons into the western mountains and to call them strangers in the immemorial home of their race. The Britons of the Roman conquest, who became the Welsh of the baffled Saxon invaders, and are the Cymry of their own history and poetry, still stand five feet four in their stockings, where they have stood from the dawn of time, an inexpugnable host of dark little men, defying the Saeseneg in their unintelligible, imperishable speech.

W. D. Howells

I

Of course, except in the loneliest and farthest places, they speak English as well as Welsh; and they misplace their aspirates, which they lost under the Normans as the Saxons did. But this did not happen to them by conquest as it did to the Saxons; they were beguiled of their h's when they were cheated with a Welsh-born prince instead of the Welsh prince they were promised in the succession of their ancient lines. They had been devout Christians, after their manner, in the earliest centuries; as the prefix Llan, or Saint, everywhere testifies, the country abounded in saints, whose sons inherited their saintship; and at the Reformation they became Calvinists as unqualifiedly as their kindred, the Bretons, remained Catholics. They have characterized the English and Americans with their strong traits in a measure which can be dimly traced in the spread of their ten or twenty national names, and they have kept even with the most modern ideals quite to the verge of co-education in their colleges. It is a fact which no Welshman will deny that Cromwell was of Welsh blood. Shakespeare was unquestionably of Welsh origin. Henry VII. was that Welsh Twdwr (or Tudor, as the Saeseneg misspell it), who set aside the Plantagenet succession, and was the grandsire of "the great Elizabeth," not to boast of Bloody Mary or Henry VIII. But if these are not enough, there is the present Chancellor of the Exchequer, Mr. Lloyd-George, who is now the chief figure of the English cabinet.

The bad name which their own half-countryman, Giraldus Cambrensis, gave the Welsh in the twelfth century, clings to them yet in the superstition of all Norman-minded and Saxon-minded men, so that the Englishman I met on the way from Edinburgh was doubtless speaking racially rather than personally when he said that the Welsh were the prize liars of the universe. I for my part heard no lies in Wales except those I told myself; but as I am of Welsh stock, perhaps my experience is not wholly refutive of that Englishman's position. I can only urge further the noted philological fact that the Welsh language is so full of imagery that it is almost impossible to express in it the brute veracities in which the English speech is so apt. Otherwise I should say that nowhere have I been used with a more immediate and constant sincerity than in Wales. The people were polite and they were almost always amiable, but in English, at least, they did not say the thing that was not; and their politeness was without the servile forms from lower to higher which rather weary one in England. They said "Yes," and "No," but as gently as if they had always added "Sir." If I have it on my conscience to except from my sweeping praise of sincerity the expressman at Aberystwyth who promised that our baggage should be at our lodgings in an hour, and did not bring it in five, I must add that we arrived on the last day of a great agricultural fair, when even the New York Transfer Company might have given a promise of more than wonted elasticity.

In the station of Aberystwyth there were about three or four thousand Welshmen of the national height, volubly waiting for the trains to bear them away to their farms and villages; but they made way most amiably for the dismounting travellers, who in our case were led through them by the most energetic porter I ever knew. They did not stare down upon us from the unseemly altitude of other national statures, and often during our stay I saw like crowds of civil men in the street markets who were no taller, and sometimes there were women who had not scaled the heights reached by our American girls. They would probably have competed fairly well with these in the courses of the colleges to which the Welsh send their daughters as well as their sons; but I will not pretend that the good looks of either the men or women was of the American average. I cannot even say that these contemporary ancient Britons had the advantage of the toothless English peasantry in the prompt dentistry which is our peculiar blessing. In Great Britain, though I must not say Ireland, for I have never been there, a few staggering incisors seem a formidable equipment of the jaw in lower-class middle life and even tender youth. The difference is a tremendous advantage which, if it does not make for the highest character in us, will doubtless stand us in good stead in any close with the well-toothed Japanese, and when we are beaten, our gold-fillings will go far to pay our indemnity.

After all those thousands at the station had departed, there were still visitors enough left in Aberystwyth to distend the hotels uncomfortably; and the next morning we set out in the pursuit, always interesting and alluring, of lodgings. The town seemed to be pretty full of lodgings, but as it was the middle of August, and the very height of the season, they were full-up in dismaying measure. We found the only one not kept by a Welsh woman in the ostensible keeping of an Englishwoman, a veteran cockney landlady, but behind her tottering throne reigned a Welsh girl, under whose iron rule we fell as if we had been unworthy Saeseneg instead of Cymric-fetched Americans. We had rejected other lodgings because, though their keepers had promised to provision us, it always appeared that we must go out and do the marketing ourselves. I shall lastingly regret that we did not submit to this condition, for it would have been one of the best means of studying the local life. But we held out for the London custom, and before the Welsh Power, which has so often made itself felt behind English thrones, could intervene, compliance was promised. After that it remained for the Welsh Power to make our stay difficult, and our going easy.

Otherwise the place was delightful; it was in almost the centre of the long curve of the Victoria Terrace, with windows that looked down upon the pebbly beach, and over the blue sea to the bluer stretch of the Pembrokeshire hills on the south, and the Carnarvonshire hills on the north, holding the lovely waters in their shadowy embrace. There was not much shipping, and what there was seemed of the pleasure sort that parties go down to the sea to be sick in. The long parade was filled at most hours with the English who make the place their resort; whose bathing began early in the morning and whose flirting continued far into the night, with forenoon and afternoon dawdling and dozing on the pebbles. At one end of the Terrace rose a prodigious headland, whose slope was scaled over with broken slate, like some mammoth heaving from the deep and showing an elephantine hide of bluish gray. At the other end was the Amusement Pier, with the co- educational college, which is part of the University of Wales, and with divers hotels. Somewhat behind and beyond were the ruins of one of those castles which the Normans planted with a mailed fist at every vantage in Wales, as their sole means of holding down the swarming, squirming,

W. D. Howells

fighting little dark people of the country. Even then they could not do it, for the Welsh, often overrun, were never conquered, as they will tell you themselves if you ask them. But Wales is now perhaps the most peaceful country in the world. Its prisons for the most part stand empty (it is said), and the people, once so turbulent, are as little given to violence as to vice. In fact, I once heard a great Welsh scholar declare that in the old times it was not the true Welsh who kept up the fighting, either on the public or the private scale, but the Scotch and Irish who had found a home among them. In any case, it is true that after the Normans had planted their castles in Wales to hold the country, it was all they could do to hold the castles, and not till their enemies had imagined having the English King's son born in one of them did they bring the Welsh under the English crown at last. Even then that uncertain people broke from their allegiance now and again; or the Scotch and Irish among them did.

III

All sorts of sights and sounds might be expected on our
Terrace, but that which especially warmed the heart of exile
in us, and pleased the fancy of other sojourners was the
appearance, one evening, of a stately band of tall men in
evening dress and top- hats, with musical instruments in their
grasp, and heads lifted high above their Welsh following. We
called the Power behind the Throne to the window in our
question and she gave a glad cry: "Oh, they're the Neegurs!
They're the white Neegurs!" and at sight of our compatriotic
faces at the pane, these beautiful giants took their stand
before our house, and burst into the familiar music of the
log-cabin, the stern-wheel steamboat, and the cornfield, as
well as the ragtime melodies of later days. It was a rich
moment, and I know not which joyed in it more, the Welsh
Power or the American Sufferance.

But here, before I go farther afield, I must note a main
difference between the Welsh Power and the English slavey
to whom she corresponded in calling and condition. She was
so far educated as to know the pseudonym of the friend who
came to see us, and to have read his writings in the *Welsh
Gazette*, treating our proposed triumph in his distinction with
the fine scorn she used for all our airs. If she had been an
old-fashioned Yankee Help she could not have been more
snubbing; but when we had been taught to know our place
she was more tolerant, and finally took leave of us without
rancor.

The notion of the general Welsh education which her
intelligence gave us was carried indefinitely farther by the
grocer's boy to whom our friend presented me one evening,
after he had been struggling to make me understand what an
englyn was. I am able now to explain that it is a polite stanza

which the Welsh send with a present of fruit or flowers, or for a greeting upon any worthy occasion. It is rhymed, sometimes at both ends of the lines, and sometimes in the middle of them, and it presents all the difficulties of euphony which the indomitable Welsh glory in overcoming. But when my friend took me in hand, my ignorance was of so dense a surface that he could make no impression on it, and he said at last, "Let us go into this grocery. There's a boy here who will *show* you what an englyn is," and after I was introduced the kind youth did so with pleasure, while he sold candles to one customer, soap to another, cheese to another, and herring to another. He first wrote the englyn in Welsh, and when I had sufficiently admired it in that tongue (for which no atavistic knowledge really served me), he said he would put it into English, and he did so. It was then not rhymed at both ends or in the middle, but it was rhymed quite enough, and if it had not the harp-like sweetness of the original, it was still such a musical stanza that I shall always be sorry to have lost it. What I can never lose the impression of is the wide-spread literary lore of the common Welsh people which the incident suggested. I could not fancy even a Boston grocer's boy doing the like; and perhaps this was an uncommon boy in Wales itself. He told me a good deal, which I have mainly forgotten, about the state of polite learning in his country and in what honor the living bards were held. It seems that in that rhyming and singing little land, the poets are still known as of old by their bardic names. As Jones, or Evans, or Edwards they have no fame beyond other men, but up and down all Wales they are celebrated as this bard or that, and are honored according to their poetic worth.

IV

After the appearance of the White Neegurs on the Terrace, I could hardly have expected any livelier appeal to my American pride, and yet it came, one day, when I learned that the line of carriages which I saw passing our windows were the vehicles bearing to some public function the members of the British Chautauqua. How far the name and idea of Chautauqua have since spread there is no saying, but it was the last of our national inventions which I should have expected to find in Aberystwyth, though Welsh culture was reasonably in its line, and the Eisteddfod was not out of keeping with the summer conferences held beside our lovely up-State lake. The British Chautauqua, as I saw it, was a group of people from all parts of the United Kingdom joined in the pursuit of improvement and enjoyment, and they were now here on one of their summer outings. They had been invited to a gentleman's place not far from Aberystwyth to view as indubitable a remnant of the Holy Grail as now exists, and it was my very good fortune through the kind offices of that friend of ours to be invited with them.

It was a blamelessly rainless afternoon, of a sort commoner on the western Welsh coast than on other shores of the "rainy isles," but not too common even there; and we drove out of the town through the prettiest country of hillside fields and valleys opening to the sea, on a road that was fairly dusty in the hot sun. There were cottages, grouped and detached, all the way, with gray stone walls and blue slate roofs, and in places the children ran out from them with mercenary offerings of flowers and song, or with frank pleas for charity direct. I yielded with reluctance to the instruction of a Manchester economist in my carriage, and denied them, when I would so much rather have abetted them in their wicked attempts on our pockets. I remember ruefully still

W. D. Howells

that they had voices as sweet and eyes as dark as the children who used to chase our wheels in Italy, and I have no doubt they deserved quite as well of us as those did.

I got back my spirits when we left our carriages, and I found myself walking up a pleasant avenue of wilding trees, with a young Chautauquan from Australia who looked as if he might be a young Chautauquan from Alabama, tall, and lean, and brown. We fell into talk about the trees, and he said how they differed in their green from the sombre gray of his native forests; and then he, from that vast far continent of his, spoke of the little island where we were, as Home. That has always a strange effect for us self-outcasts from the great British roof, and whether it makes us smile, or makes us sigh, it never fails to startle us when we hear it from colonial lips. The word holds in common kindness Canada and India and South Africa and Australia, and it has its pathos in the fact that the old mother of these mighty children seems to leave solely to them the tenderness that draws them to her in that notion of home.

V

There were about fifty of those British Chautauquans, and when they had ranged themselves on the grass before the shrubbery of a pleasant lawn, backed by a wooded slope, the dignified lady of the house came out with a casket in her hand, and put it on a table, and the exercises began. Fitly, if the casket really held the sacred relic, they began with prayer; then a Welsh soloist followed with a hymn, but whether she sang in Welsh or English, I do not remember; I am only sure she sang divinely; and then came the speeches. The first of the speeches was by our friend, who was the local Unitarian minister, and of a religious body not inconsiderable in that Calvinistic Wales. He told us how the Holy Grail had been deposited with the monks of Strata Florida, the famous old abbey near Aberystwyth; but I forgot who made them this trust, unless it was King Arthur's knights, and I am not sure whether the fact is matter of legend or history. What I remember is that when the abbey was suppressed by Henry VIII., certain of the escaping monks came with the relic to the gentle house where we then were, and placed it in the keeping of the family who have guarded it ever since.

After our friend, the lady of this house took up the tale, and told in words singularly choice and simple the story of the sacred relic as the family knew it. I had only once before heard a woman speak, no less a woman than our great and dear Julia Ward Howe, and it seemed to me that she spoke better than any man; and I must say of the Chautauquans' hostess, that day, that if ever the Englishwomen come into their full political rights, as they seem sure to do, the traditions of good sense and good taste in English public speaking will not pass, but will prosper on through their orators. There were touches of poetry, nationally Welsh, in

W. D. Howells

what she said, and touches of humor perhaps personally Welsh. It seems that the cup had been famed throughout the countryside for the miraculous property by which whoever drank from it was cured of his or her malady, and it had been passed freely round to all sufferers ever since it came into her family's keeping. That they might make doubly sure of the miracle, it was the custom of the sick not only to empty the cup, but to nibble a little bit of the wood, and swallow that, so that in whatever state the monks of Strata Florida had confided it, the vessel was now in the state we saw. Saying this the lady opened the casket holding it, and showed us the crescent-shaped rim of a wooden bowl, about the bigness of a cocoanut shell; all the rest had been consumed by the pious sufferers whom it had restored to health.

I am sorry, after all, to own that this cup is said by some authorities not to be the Holy Grail, but a vessel like it carved out of the true cross. But even so subordinate a relic is priceless, and as it is no longer possible to drink from it, we may hope that the fragment will remain indefinitely to after time. When they had wondered at the sight of it the Chautauquans and their friend were made free of the charming seventeenth-century house, which would be old for this country, but which in the taste of that time was rather modern, and looked like the casino of some Italian villa. It abounded, as such houses in England do, in the pictured faces of the past, and in the memorials which only the centuries can leave behind them, but was too graceful to seem rich. "A home of ancient peace," it looked, in its mild gray stone amidst its lawns and shrubberies, the larger hold of the gardens and pleasaunces through which the Chautauquans followed from it.

VI

At Aberystwyth, and elsewhere in Wales, one of the things I noticed was the difference of the people from the people over the English border in their attitude toward their betters. They might stand only five feet in their stockings, but they stood straight, and if they were respectful, they were first self-respectful. In our run from Shrewsbury, their language first made itself generally heard at Newport, and it increased in the unutterable names of the stations westward, the farther we passed into their beautiful country, but they had always English enough to be civil, though never servile. The country is beautiful in the New England measure, but it is of a softer and smaller beauty; it looks more caressable; it is like Vermont rather than New Hampshire, and it is more like New England than Old England in the greater number of isolated farm-houses, from which the girls as well as the boys come to the university colleges for learning undreamt of by English farm villagers.

The air was fresh and sweet, and though it seemed to shower wherever we stopped to let another train go by on a siding of our single track, there was a very passable sense of summer sun. The human type as we began to observe it and as we saw it afterward throughout the land was not only diminutive, but rather plain and mostly dark, in the men; as to the women they were, as they are everywhere, charming, with now and then a face of extraordinary loveliness, and nearly always the exquisite West of England complexion. In their manners the people could not be more amiable than the English, who are as amiable as possible, but they seemed brighter and gayer. This remained their effect to the last in Aberystwyth, and when one left the Terrace where the English visitors superabounded, the Welsh had the whole place to themselves. I would not push my conjecture, but it

W. D. Howells

seemed to me that there was an absence of the cloying loyalty which makes sojourn in England afflictive to the republican spirit; I remember but one shop dedicated to the King's Majesty, with the royal arms over the door, though there may have been many others; I am always warning the reader not to take me too literally.

Though I was about the streets by day and by dark, I saw no disorderly behavior of any kind in the town away from the beach; I do not mean there was any by the sea, unless some athletic courtship among the young people of the watering-place element was to be accounted so. There was not much fashion there, except in a few pretty women who recalled the church parade of Hyde Park in their flowery and feathery costumes. Back in the town there was no fashion at all, but a general decency and comfort of dress. The Welsh costume survives almost solely in the picture-postal cards, though perhaps in the hilly fastnesses the women still wear the steeple-crowned hats which we associate with the notion of witches; when they come to market in Aberystwyth they wear hard, shiny black straw hats like the men's. Amongst the throng of Saturday-night shoppers I saw none of the drunkenness that one sees so often in Scottish streets, and in English cities, and, I grieve to say, even in some New England towns. In the Welsh quarter Sunday was much more the Sabbath than it was on the Terrace, where indeed it seemed a day of pleasure rather than praise.

VII

All the week I had the best intention of hearing the singing in some of the Welsh churches, but my goodwill could not carry the day against the fear of a sermon which I should not understand. A chance sermon would probably have touched upon the education act which was then stirring all Dissenting England and Wales to passive resistance, and from Lincolnshire to Carnarvonshire was causing the distraint of tables and chairs, tools, hams, clocks, clothing, poultry, and crops for the payment of such part of the Dissenters' taxes as would go to the support of the Church schools. Possibly it might also have referred to the Walk Out of the Welsh Members of Parliament; this was an incident which I heard mentioned as of imperial importance, though what caused it or came of it I do not know.

Instead of going to church, I strolled up and down the Terrace and observed the watering-place life. The town was evidently full, or at least all the lodging-houses were, and as it is with the English everywhere in their summer resorts, there were men enough to go round, so that no poor dear need pine for a mate on that pleasant beach. Aberystwyth is therefore to be commended to our overflow of girls, though whether there are many eligible noblemen among those youth I have not the statistics for saying. All the visitors may have been people of rank; I only know that I was told they were mostly from the midland cities, and they seemed to be having the good time which people of brief outings alone have. The bathing began, as I have noted, very early in the day with the men in the briefest possible tights; the women, for compensation, wore long trousers with their bathing-skirts, and they enhanced the modesty of their effect by the universal use of bathing-machines, pushed well away from the curious shore. There was not much variety in the visiting

W. D. Howells

English type, but there was here and there a sharp imperial accent, as in the two pale little, spindle-legged Anglo-Indian boys, with their Hindu ayah, very dark, with sleek dark hair, and gleaming eyes in a head not much bigger than a black walnut.

The crescent of the beach was a serried series of hotels and lodging-houses, from tip to tip, but back of these were streets of homelike, smallish dwellings, that broke rank farther away, and scattered about in suburban villas, with trees and flowers and grass around them. Beyond stretched, as well as it could stretch among its hills, the charming country of fields, and woods, and orchards.

VIII

I suppose I did not quite do my duty by the ruins of the Norman castle, and I feel that it is now too late to repair my neglect. The stronghold was more than once attempted by the Welsh in those wars which make their history a catalogue of battles, but it held out Norman till the Normans turned English. Owen Glendover took it in 1402, when it was three hundred years old, though not yet feeble with age, and in due time one of Cromwell's lieutenants destroyed it. Some very picturesque fragments remain to attest the grace and strength of the ancient hold. It is near the University College and the Amusement Pier, so that the mere sight-seers can do all the ordinary objects of interest at Aberystwyth in half a day or half an hour. But we were none of these. We had fallen in love with the place, and we would fain have stayed on after the week was up for which we had taken our lodging. It appeared from a house-to-house canvass, that there was no other lodging to be had in all that long crescent of the Terrace; or, if this is incredible, there was none we would have. Our successors were impending; and though I think our English landlady might have invented something for us at the last moment, the Welsh Power was inexorable. Her ideal was lodgers who would go out and buy their own provisions, and we had set our faces against that. Some one must yield, and the Welsh Power could not; it was not in her nature. We were therefore in a manner expelled from Aberystwyth, but our banishment was not from all Wales, and this was how we went next to Llandudno.

* * * * *

W. D. Howells

LLANDUDNO, ANOTHER WELSH WATERING-PLACE

Froissart's saying, if it was Froissart's, that the English amuse themselves sadly antedates that notion of Merry England which is now generally rejected by serious observers. I should myself prefer the agnostic position, and say that I did not know whether the English were glad or not when they looked gay. What I seem to be certain of, but I do not say that I am certain, is that they look gayer in their places of amusement than we do. I do not mean theatres, or parliaments, or music-halls, or lecture-rooms, by places of amusement, but what we call summer resorts a little more largely than those resorts which the English call watering-places. Of these I should like to take as a type the charming summer resort on the coast of North Wales which is called Llandudno in print, and in speech several different ways.

I

The English simply and frankly, after their blunt nature, call the place Landudno, but the Welsh call it, according to one superstition of their double *l* and their French *u*, Thlandidno. According to another, we cannot spell it in English at all; but it does not much matter, for the last superstition is the ever-delightful but ever-doubtful George Borrow's, who says that the Welsh *ll* is the same as the Spanish *ll*, but who is probably mistaken, most other authorities agreeing that if you pronounce it *lhl* you will come as near it as any Saeseneg need. It is a constantly besetting question in Wales, where the prefix *Llan* speckles the map all over, owing to that multitude of Saints who peopled the country in the times when a Saint's sons were every one saints, and none was of particularly holy, or even good life, because he was known for a saint. Like a continental noble, he inherited his title equally with all his brothers.

But through whatever orthoepic mazes you search it, Llandudno has every claim on your regard and admiration. Like Aberystwyth, its sea front is a shallow crescent, but vaster, with a larger town expanding back of it, and with loftier and sublimer headlands, at either end, closing it in a more symmetrical frame. But I should say that its sea was not so blue, or its sky either, and its air was not so soft or dry. Morally it is more constantly lively, with a greater and more insistent variety of entertainments. For the American its appeal might well have begun with the sight of his country's flag floating over a tennis-ground at the neighboring watering-place and purer Welsh town of Rhyl. The approach to his affections was confirmed by another American flag displayed before one of the chief hotels in Llandudno itself. I learned afterward of the landlord that this was because there were several Chicago families in his

W. D. Howells

house, and fifteen Americans in all; but why the tennis-ground of Rhyl flew our national banner, I do not know to this day. It was indeed that gentle moment when our innocent people believed themselves peculiarly dear to the English, and might naturally suppose, if from Chicago, or Boston, or Denver, that the English would wish to see as often as possible the symbol of our successful revolt from the princes and principles to which they have religiously adhered.

Both that home of the patriotic Chicago families, and the other best hotel were too full for us, and after a round of the second-best we decided for lodgings, hoping as usual that they would bring us nearer the native life. The best we could get, facing the sea midway of the crescent, were not exactly Welsh in their keeping. The landladies were, in fact, two elderly Church-of- England sisters from Dublin, who had named their house out of a novel they had read. They said they believed the name was Italian, and the reader shall judge if it were so from its analogue of Osier Wood. The maids in the house, however, were very truly and very wickedly Welsh: two tough little ponies of girls, who tied their hair up with shoe-strings, and were forbidden, when about their work, to talk Welsh together, lest they should speak lezing of those Irish ladies. The rogues were half English, but the gentle creature who served our table was wholly Welsh; small, sweet-voiced, dark-eyed, intelligent, who suffered from the universal rheumatism of the British Isles, but kept steadily to her duty, and accepted her fate with patience and even cheerfulness. She waited on several other tables, for the house was full of lodgers, all rather less permanent than ourselves, who were there for a fortnight; we found our landladies hoping, when we said we were going, to have had us with them through the winter.

II

Our fellow-lodgers were quiet people of divers degrees, except perhaps the highest, unless the nobility bring boiled hams with them when they visit the seaside. The boiled ham of the drawing- room floor was frankly set out on the hall table, where it seemed to last a week, or at least till the lodgers went away. There was much coming and going, for it was the height of the season, with the prices at flood tide. We paid six guineas a week for three bedrooms and a sitting-room; but our landladies owned it was dear. An infirm and superannuated sideboard served for a dressing-table in one room; in others the heavier pieces of furniture stood sometimes on four legs, sometimes on three. We had the advantage of two cats on the back fence, and a dog in the back yard; but if the controversy between them was carried on in Welsh, it is no wonder we never knew what it was about.

Our hostesses said the Welsh were dirty housekeepers: "At least *we* think so," but I am bound to say their own cooking was very good; and not being Welsh our hostesses consented to market for us, except in the article of Spanish melons: these I bought myself of increasing cost and size. When I alleged, the second morning, that the melon then sold me for sixpence had been sold me by another boy for fourpence the day before, my actual Cymric youth said, "Then he asked you too little," which seemed a *non sequitur* but was really an unexpected stroke of logic.

It was the utmost severity used with me by my co-racials in Llandudno. They were in the great majority of the permanent inhabitants, but they were easily outnumbered among the pleasurers by the Saeseneg, whose language prevailed, so that a chance word of Welsh now and then was all that I

W. D. Howells

heard in the streets. Some faint stirrings of ambition to follow the language as far as a phrase-book would lead were not encouraged by the kindly bookseller who took my money for it; and I did not go on. It is a loss for me in literature which translation cannot supply, for the English lovers of Welsh poetry, after praising it to the skies, are never able to produce anything which is not direly mechanical and vacuous. The native charm somehow escapes them; the grace beyond the reach of art remains with the Cymric poets who have resources for its capture unknown to their English admirers. George Borrow seems the worst failure in this sort, and the worst offender in giving his reader the hopes he never fulfils, so that his *Wild Wales* is a desert of blighted literary promises. I believe that the merit of Welsh poetry dwells largely, perhaps overlargely, in its intricate technique, and in the euphonic changes which leave the spoken word ready for singing almost without the offices of the composer.

III

One of the great musical contests, the yearly national Eisteddfod, was taking place that year at the neighboring town of Rhyl, but I did not go to hear it, not being good for a week's music without intermission. At Llandudno there was only the music of the Pierrots and the Niggers, which those simple-hearted English have borrowed, the one from France and the other from these States. Their passion for our colored minstrelsy is, in fact, something pathetic. They like Pierrots well enough, and Pierrots *are* amusing, there is no doubt of it; but they dote upon Niggers, as they call them with a brutality unknown among us except to the vulgarest white men and boys, and the negroes themselves in moments of exasperation. Negro minstrelsy is almost extinct in the land of its birth, but in the land of its adoption it flourishes in the vigor of undying youth: no watering-place is genuine without it. Bands of Niggers haunt the streets and suburbs of London, and apparently every high day or holiday through-out the British Islands requires the stamp of their presence as a nostrum requires the name of the patentee blown in the bottle. The decay of their gay science began among us with the fall of slavery, and the passing of the old plantation life; but as these never existed in Great Britain the English version of negro minstrelsy is not affected by their disapp-earance. It is like the English tradition of the Red Skins, which has all but vanished from our superstition, but remains as powerful as ever in the constant fancy of those islanders.

The English like their Niggers very, very black, and as their Niggers are English they know how to gratify the national preference: such a spread of scarlet lips over half the shining sable face is known nowhere else in nature or art; and it must have been in despair of rivalling their fellow-minstrels that the small American troupe we saw at Aberystwyth went to

　　　　　W. D. Howells

the opposite extreme and frankly appeared as the White Neegurs. At Llandudno the blackness of the Niggers was absolute, so that it almost darkened the day as they passed our lodging, along the crescent of the beach on their way to their open-air theatre beyond it. They were followed by a joyous retinue of boys and girls, tradesmen's apprentices, donkeys, bath-chairs, and all the movable gladness of the watering-place, to the music of their banjos and the sound of their singing. They were going to a fold of the foot-hills called the Happy Valley, bestowed on the public for such pleasures by the local nobleman whose title is given to a principal street, and to other points and places, I suppose out of the public pride and gratitude. It is a charming amphitheatre overlooked by the lofty tops around, and there on the green slope the Niggers had set up their stage, and ranged the spectators' chairs in the classification of first, second, and third so dear to the British soul. There they cracked their jokes, and there they sang their songs; the songs were newer than the jokes, but they were both kinds delivered with a strong Cockney accent, and without an aspirate in its place. But it was all richly acceptable to the audience, who laughed and cheered and joined in the chorus when asked. Here, as everywhere, the crowd delighted equally in songs of the sloppiest sentimentality and of humor nighest indecency.

On the afternoon of our visit the good lady next me could not contain her peculiar pride in the entertainment, and confided that she knew the leader of the troupe, who was an old friend of her husband's. It was indeed a time and place that invited to expansion. Nothing could have been friendlier and livelier than the spectacle of the spectators spread over the grassy slope, or sublimer than the rise of the hills around, or more enchanting than the summer sea, with the large and little shipping on it, and the passenger-steamers going and coming from Liverpool and all the points in the region round. The two headlands which mark the limits of the beautiful beach, Great Orme's Head, and Little Orme's Head, are both of a nobleness tempered to kindliness by the soft and manageable beauty of their forms. I never got quite so far as Little Orme's Head, for it was full two miles from our lodging, and a fortnight was not long enough for the journey, but with Great Orme's Head I was on terms of very tolerable intimacy. A road of the excellence peculiar to England passes round on the chin, so to speak, and though I never went the length of it, I went far enough to know the majesty of the seaward prospect. From the crown of the Head there is a view of perhaps all the mountains in Wales, which from this point appears entirely composed of mountains, blue, blue and enchantingly fair. On the townward side you may descend into the Happy Valley, as we did, and find always a joyous crowd listening to the Niggers. If, after some doubt of your way, you have the favor of a nice boy and an intelligent collie dog, whom the boy is helping herd home the evening cows of a pleasant farm, you will have a charming glimpse of the local civilization; and perhaps you will notice that the cows do not pay much attention to the boy, but obey the dog implicitly; it is their Old World convention.

W. D. Howells

IV

From another side we had ascended the mountain by the tram line which climbs it to the top, and at every twist and turn lavishes some fresh loveliness of landscape upon your vision. Near by, we noticed many depressions and sinkages in the ground, and a conversable man in well-oiled overalls who joined us at a power- house, said it was from the giving way of the timbers in the disused copper-mines. Were they very old, we asked, and he said they had not been worked for forty years; but this, when you come to think of the abandoned Roman mines yet deeper in the hill, was a thing of yesterday. The man in the oily overalls had evidently not come to think of it, but he was otherwise a very intelligent mechanic, and of a hospitable mind, like all the rest of our chance acquaintance in Great Britain. I do not know that I like to think of those Roman mines myself, where it is said the sea now surges back and forth: they must have been worked by British slaves, who may be fancied climbing purblindly out when the legions left Britain, and not joining very loudly in the general lamentation at their withdrawal, but probably tempering the popular grief with the reflection that the heathen Saxons could not be much worse.

The hill-top was covered with the trippers who seem perpetually holidaying on their island, and who were always kind to their children when they had them, and to each other when they had not. They were commonly in couples, very affectionate and inoffensively young. They wandered about, and from time to time went and had tea at one of the tea-houses which are always at hand over there. Except the view there was not much to see; the ways were rough; now and then you came to a pink cottage or a white one where the peasantry, again, sold tea. At one place in our walk over the occiput of Great Orme's Head into the Happy Valley in its bosom, we fell a prey to a conspiracy of boys selling mignonette: it appeared to be a mignonette trust, or syndicate, confining its commerce to that flower.

I have no other statistics to offer concerning business on Great Orme's Head, or indeed in all Llandudno. One of the chief industries seemed to be coaching, for a score of delightful places are to be easily reached by the stages always departing from the hotels on the Parade. There was no particularly noticeable traffic in leek, though I suppose that as I did not see the national emblem in any Welshman's hat—to be sure, it was not St. David's Day—it must have been boiling in every Welshman's pot. I am rather ashamed to be joining, even at this remove, in the poor English joking which goes on about the Welsh, quite as much as about the Scotch, the Irish having become too grave a matter for joking. There are little burlesque manuals making merry with the language and its agglutinative prolixity, which I shall certainly not quote; and there are postal-cards representing Welsh dames drinking tea in tall witch-hats, with one of them saying: "I wass enjoying myself shocking, look you." There was, of course, nothing serious in this joking; the Welsh, who have all the small commerce in their hands, gladly sold the manuals and postals, and I did not see one Englishman laughing over them.

The Saeseneg visitors rather amused themselves with the sea and the resources of the beach and the bathing. As contrasted with the visitors at Aberystwyth, so distinctly in the earlier and later stages of love-making, I should say those at Llandudno were domestic: fathers and mothers who used the long phalanx of bathing-machines appointed to their different sexes, and their children who played in the sand. I thought the children charming, and I contributed tuppence to aid in the repair of the sand castle of two nice little boys which had fallen down; it now seems strange that I should have been asked for a subscription, but in England subscriptions spare nobody; though I wonder if two such nice little boys would have come to me for money in America. Besides the entertainment of lying all afternoon on the beach, or sitting beside it in canopied penny chairs, there was more active diversion for all ages and sexes in the circus prevailing somewhere in the background, and advertising itself every afternoon by a procession of six young elephants neatly carrying each in his trunk the tail of the elephant before him. There were also the delightful shows of the amusement pier where one could go and see Pierrots to one's heart's content, if one can ever get enough of Pierrots; I never can.

Besides all these daytime things there were two very good theatres, at one of which I saw Mr. Barrie's *Little Mary* given better than in New York (that was easy), and at the other a comic opera, with a bit of comedy or tragedy in a stage-box, not announced in the bills. The audience was otherwise decorous enough to be composed of Welsh Baptist elders and their visiting friends, but in this box there were two young men in evening dress, scuffling with a young woman in dinner decolletee, and what appeared to be diamonds in her ears. They were trying, after what seems the convention of English seaside flirtation, to get something out of her hand, and allowing her successfully to resist them; and their playful contest went on through a whole act to the distraction of the spectators, who did not seem greatly scandalized. It suggested the misgiving that perhaps bad people came to Llandudno for their summer outing as well as good; but there was no interference by the police or the management with this robust side-show. Were the actors in the scene, all or any of them, too high in rank to be lightly molested in their lively event; or were they too low? Perhaps they were merely tipsy, but all the same their interlude was a contribution to the evening's entertainment which would not have been so placidly accepted in, say, Atlantic City, or Coney Island, or even Newport, where people are said to be more accustomed to the caprices of society persons, and more indulgent of their whims.

W. D. Howells

V

A more improving, and on the whole more pleasing, phase of the indigenous life, and also more like a phase of our own, showed itself the day of our visit to Conway, a little way from Llandudno. There, on our offering to see the ruins of the wonderful and beautiful old castle, we were met at the entrance with a demand for an exceptional shilling gate money, because of the fair for the local Wesleyan Chapel which was holding in the interior. What seemed at first a hardship turned out a chance which we would not have missed on any account. There was a large tent set up in the old castle court, and a table spread with home-made dainties of many sorts, and waited upon by gentle maids and matrons who served one with tea or whatever else one liked, all for that generously inclusive shilling. They were Welsh, they told us, and they were speaking their language to right and left of us, while they were so courteous to us in English. It was quite like a church fair in some American village, where, however, it could not have had the advantage of a ruined Norman castle for its scene, and where it would not have provided a range for target practice with air-guns, or grounds for running and jumping.

The place was filled with people young and old who were quietly amusing themselves and were more taken up with the fair than with the castle. I must myself comparatively slight the castle in the present study of people rather than places, though I may note that if there is any more interesting ruin in the world, I am satisfied with this which it surpasses. Besides its beauty, what strikes one most is its perfect adaptation to the original purpose of palace and fortress for which the Normans planned their strongholds in Wales. The architect built not only with a constant instinct of beauty, but with unsurpassable science and skill. The skill and the science have gone the way of the need of them, but the beauty remains indelible and as eternal as the hunger for it in the human soul. Conway castle is not all a ruin, even as a fortress, however. Great part of it still challenges decay, and is so entire in its outward shape that it has inspired the railway running under its shoulder to attempt a conformity of style in the bridge approaching it, but without enabling it to an equal effect of grandeur. One would as soon the bridge had not tried.

All Conway is worthy, within its ancient walls, of as much devotion as one can render it in the rain, which begins as soon as you leave the castle. The walls climb from the waters to the hills, and the streets wander up and down and seem to the stranger mainly to seek that beautiful old Tudor house, Plas Mawr, which like the castle is without rival in its kind. It was full of reeking and streaming sight-seers, among whom one could easily find one's self incommoded without feeling one's self a part of the incommodation, but in spite of them there was the assurance of comfort as well as splendor in the noble old mansion, such as the Elizabethan houses so successfully studied. In the dining-room a corner of the mantel has its sandstone deeply worn away, and a much-elbowed architect, who was taking measurements of the chimney, agreed that this carf was the effect of the host or the butler flying to the place and sharpening his knife for whatever haunch of venison or round of beef was toward. It was a fine memento of the domestic past, and there was a secret chamber where the refugees of this cause or that in other times were lodged in great discomfort. Besides, there was a ghost which was fairly crowded out of its accustomed quarters, where so far from being able to walk, it would have had much ado to stand upright by flattening itself against the wall.

W. D. Howells

VI

In fact, there was not much more room that day in the Plas Mawr, than in the Smallest House in the World, which is the next chiefest attraction of Conway. This, too, was crammed with damp enthusiasts, passionately eager to sign their names in the guest- book. They scarcely left space in the sitting-room of ten by twelve feet for the merry old hostess selling photographs and ironically inviting her visitors' guests to a glimpse of the chamber overhead, or so much of it as the bed allowed to be seen. She seemed not to believe in her abode as a practicable tenement, and could not be got to say that she actually lived in it; as to why it was built so small she was equally vague. But there it was, to like or to leave, and there, not far off, was the "briny beach" where the Walrus and the Carpenter walked together,—

"And wept like anything to see
Such quantities of sand."

For it was in Conway, as history or tradition is, that *Through the Looking-Glass* was written.

There are very few places in those storied British Isles which are not hallowed by some association with literature; but I suppose that Llandudno is as exempt as any can be, and I will not try to invoke any dear and honored shade from its doubtful obscurity. We once varied the even tenor of our days there by driving to Penmaenmawr, and wreaking our love of literary associations so far as we might by connecting the place with the memory of Gladstone, who was literary as well as political. We thought with him that Penmaenmawr was "the most charming watering-place in Wales," and as you drive into the place, the eye of faith will detect the house, on the right, in which he spent many happy summers.

We contented ourselves with driving direct to the principal hotel, where I know not what kept us from placing ourselves for life. We had tea and jam en the pretty lawn, and the society of a large company of wasps of the yellow- jacket variety, which must have been true Welsh wasps, as peaceful as they were musical, and no interloping Scotch or Irish, for they did not offer to attack us, but confined themselves altogether to our jam: to be sure, we thought best to leave it to them.

It is said that the purple year is not purpler at any point on the southernmost shores of England than it is at Llandudno. In proof of the mildness of its winter climate, the presence of many sorts of tender evergreens is alleged, and the persistence of flowers in blooming from Christmas to Easter. But those who have known the deceitful habits of flowers on the Riviera, where they bloom in any but an arctic degree of cold, will not perhaps hurry to Llandudno much later than November. All the way to Penmaenmawr the flowers showed us what they could do in summer, whether in field or garden, and there was one beautiful hill on which immense sweeps and slopes of yellow gorse and purple heather boldly stretched separately, or mingled their dyes in the fearlessness of nature when she spurns the canons of art. I suppose there is no upholsterer or paperhanger who would advise mixing or matching yellow and purple in the decoration of a room, but here the outdoor effect rapt the eye in a transport of delight. It was indeed a day when almost any arrangement of colors would have pleased.

W. D. Howells

VII

It is not easy in that much summer-resorted region to get at the country in other than its wilder moods; it is either town or mountain; but now and then one found one's self among harvest-fields, where the yield of wheat and oats was far heavier than with us, either because the soil was richer or the tilth thorougher. The farms indeed looked very fertile, and the farmhouses very alluringly clean and neat, at least on the outside. They were not gray, as in the West of England, or brick as in the Southeast, but were of stone whitewashed, and the roofs were of slate, and not thatch or tile. As I have noted, they were not so much gathered into villages as in England, and again, as I have noted, it is out of such houses that the farmers' boys and girls go to the co-educational colleges of the Welsh University. It is still the preference of the farmers that their sons should be educated for the ministry, which in that country of multiplied dissents has pulpits for every color of contrary-mindedness, as well as livings of the not yet disestablished English Church. It is not indeed the English Church in speech. The Welsh will have their service and their sermon in their own tongue, and when an Oxford or Cambridge man is given a Welsh living, he must do what he can to conform to the popular demand. It is said that in one case, where the incumbent long held out against the parish, he compromised by reading the service in Welsh with the English pronunciation. But the Welsh churches are now supplied with Welsh-speaking clergy, though whether it is well for the Welsh to cling so strongly to their ancient speech is doubted by many Welshmen. These hold that it cramps and dwarfs the national genius; but in the mean time in Ireland the national genius, long enlarged to our universal English, offers the strange spectacle of an endeavor to climb back into its Gaelic shell.

I do not know whether an incident of my experience in coming from Chester to Llandudno is to be offered as an illustration of Welsh manners or of English manners. A woman of the middle rank, certainly below gentlewoman, but very personable and well dressed, got into our carriage where there was no seat for her. She was no longer young, but she was not so old as the American who offered her his seat. She refused it, but consented to sit on the hand-bag and rug which he arranged for her, and so remained till she left the train, while a half-grown boy and several young men kept their countenances and their places, not apparently dreaming of offering her a seat, or if they thought of her at all, thought she was well punished for letting the guard crowd her in upon us. By her stature and complexion she was undoubtedly Welsh, and these youth from theirs were as undoubtedly English. Perhaps, then, the incident had better be offered as an illustration of Welsh and English manners combined.

*　　*　　*　　*　　*

GLIMPSES OF ENGLISH CHARACTER

Nothing is so individual in any man as the peculiar blend of characteristics which he has inherited from his racial ancestries. The Englishman, who leaves the stamp of the most distinct personality upon others, is the most mixed, the most various, the most relative of all men. He is not English except as he is Welsh, Dutch, and Norman, with "a little Latin and less Greek" from his earliest visitors and invaders. This conception of him will indefinitely simplify the study of his nature if it is made in the spirit of the frank superficiality which I propose to myself. After the most careful scrutiny which I shall be able to give him, he will remain, for every future American, the contradiction, the anomaly, the mystery which I expect to leave him.

I

No error of the Englishman's latest invader is commoner than
the notion, which perhaps soonest suggests itself, that he is a
sort of American, tardily arriving at our kind of consciousness, with the disadvantages of an alien environment, after
apparently hopeless arrest in unfriendly conditions. The
reverse may much more easily be true; we may be a sort of
Englishmen, and the Englishman, if he comes to us and
abides with us, may become a sort of American. But that is
the affair of a possible future, and the actual Englishman is
certainly not yet any sort of American, unless, indeed, for
good and for bad, he is a better sort of Bostonian. He does
not even speak the American language, whatever outlandish
accent he uses in speaking his own. It may be said, rather too
largely, too loosely, that the more cultivated he is, the more
he will speak like a cultivated American, until you come to
the King, or the Royal Family, with whom a strong German
accent is reported to prevail. The Englishman may write
American, if he is a very good writer, but in no case does he
spell American. He prefers, as far as he remembers it, the
Norman spelling, and, the Conqueror having said "*geole*,"
the Conquered print "gaol," which the American invader
must pronounce "jail," not "gayol."

The mere mention of the Royal Family advances us to the
most marked of all the superficial English characteristics; or,
perhaps, loyalty is not superficial, but is truly of the blood
and bone, and not reasoned principle, but a passion induced
by the general volition. Whatever it is, it is one of the most
explicitly as well as the most tacitly pervasive of the English
idiosyncrasies. A few years ago—say, fifteen or twenty—it
was scarcely known in its present form. It was not known at
all with many in the time of the latest and worst of the
Georges, or the time of the happy-go-lucky sailor William;

W. D. Howells

in the earlier time of Victoria, it was a chivalrous devotion among the classes, and with the masses an affection which almost no other sovereign has inspired. I should not be going farther than some Englishmen if I said that her personal character saved the monarchy; when she died there was not a vestige of the republican dream which had remained from a sentiment for "the free peoples of antiquity" rather than from the Commonwealth. Democracy had indeed effected itself in a wide-spread socialism, but the kingship was safe in the hearts of the Queen's subjects when the Prince of Wales, who was the first of them, went about praising loyalty as prime among the civic virtues and duties. The notion took the general fancy, and met with an acceptance in which the old superstition of kings by divine right was resuscitated with the vulgar. One of the vulgar lately said to an American woman who owned that we did not yield an equal personal fealty to all our Presidents, "Oh yes, but you know that it is only your *people* that choose the President, but *God* gave us the King." Nothing could be opposed to a belief so simple, as in the churches of the eldest faith the humble worshipper could not well be told that the picture or the statue of his adoration was not itself sacred. In fact, it is not going too far, at least for a very adventurous spirit, to say that loyalty with the English is a sort of religious principle. What is with us more or less a joke, sometimes bad, sometimes good, namely, our allegiance to the powers that be in the person of the Chief Magistrate, is with them a most serious thing, at which no man may smile without loss.

I was so far from wishing myself to smile at it, that I darkled most respectfully about it, without the courage to inquire directly into the mystery. If it was often on my tongue to ask, "What is loyalty? How did you come by it? Why are you loyal?"—I felt that it would be embarrassing when it would not be offensive, and I should vainly plead in excuse that this property of theirs mystified me the more because it seemed absolutely left out of the American nature. I perceived that in the English it was not less really present because it was mixed, or used to be mixed, with scandal that the alien can do no more than hint at. That sort of abuse has long ceased, and if one were now to censure the King, or any of the Royal Family, it would be felt to be rather ill bred, and quite unfair, since royalty is in no position to reply to criticism. Even the Socialists would think it ill-mannered, though in their hearts, if not in their sleeves, they must all the while be smiling at the notion of anything sacred in the Sovereign.

W. D. Howells

II

Loyalty, like so many other things in England, is a convention to which the alien will tacitly conform in the measure of
his good taste or his good sense. It is not his affair, and in the
mean time it is a most curious and interesting spectacle; but
it is not more remarkable, perhaps, than the perfect
acquiescence in the aristocratic forms of society which hedge
the King with their divinity. We think that family counts for
much with ourselves, in New England or in Virginia; but it
counts for nothing at all in comparison with the face value at
which it is current in England. We think we are subject to
our plutocracy, when we are very much out of humor or out
of heart, in some such measure as the commoners of England
are subject to the aristocracy; but that is nonsense. A very
rich man with us is all the more ridiculous for his more
millions; he becomes a byword if not a hissing; he is the
meat of the paragrapher, the awful example of the preacher;
his money is found to smell of his methods. But in England,
the greater a nobleman is, the greater his honor. The
American mother who imagines marrying her daughter to an
English duke, cannot even imagine an English duke—say,
like him of Devonshire, or him of Northumberland, or him of
Norfolk—with the social power and state which wait upon
him in his duchy and in the whole realm; and so is it in
degree down to the latest and lowest of the baronets, and of
those yet humbler men who have been knighted for their
merits and services in medicine, in literature, in art. The
greater and greatest nobles are established in a fear which is
very like what the fear of God used to be when the common
people feared Him; and, though they are potent political
magnates, they mainly rule as the King himself does, through
the secular reverence of those beneath them for their titles
and the visible images of their state. They are wealthy men,
of course, with so much substance that, when one now and

then attempts to waste it, he can hardly do so; but their wealth alone would not establish them in the popular regard. His wealth does no such effect for Mr. Astor in England; and mere money, though it is much desired by all, is no more venerated in the person of its possessor than it is with us. It is ancestry, it is the uncontested primacy of families first in their place, time out of mind, that lays its resistless hold upon the fancy and bows the spirit before it. By means of this comes the sovereign effect in the political as well as the social state; for, though the people vote into or out of power those who vote other people into or out of the administration, it is always—or so nearly always that the exception proves the rule—family that rules, from the King down to the least attache of the most unimportant embassy. No doubt many of the English are restive under the fact; and, if one had asked their mind about it, one might have found them frank enough; but, never asking it, it was with amusement that I heard said once, as if such a thing had never occurred to anybody before, "Yes, isn't it strange that those few families should keep it all among themselves!" It was a slender female voice, lifted by a young girl with an air of pensive surprise, as at a curious usage of some realm of faery.

W. D. Howells

III

England is in fact, to the American, always a realm of faery, in its political and social constitution. It must be owned, concerning the government by family, that it certainly seems to work well. That justifies it, so far as the exclusion of the immense majority from the administration of their own affairs can be justified by anything; though I hold that the worst form of graft in office is hardly less justifiable: that is, at least, one of the people picking their pockets. But it is the universal make-believe behind all the practical virtue of the state that constitutes the English monarchy a realm of faery. The whole population, both the great and the small, by a common effort of the will, agree that there is a man or a woman of a certain line who can rightfully inherit the primacy amongst them, and can be dedicated through this right to live the life of a god, to be so worshipped and flattered, so cockered about with every form of moral and material flummery, that he or she may well be more than human not to be made a fool of. Then, by a like prodigious stroke of volition, the inhabitants of the enchanted island universally agree that there is a class of them which can be called out of their names in some sort of title, bestowed by some ancestral or actual prince, and can forthwith be something different from the rest, who shall thenceforth do them reverence, them and their heirs and assigns, forever. By this amusing process, the realm of faery is constituted, a thing which could not have any existence in nature, yet by its existence in fancy becomes the most absolute of human facts.

It is not surprising that, in the conditions which ensue, snobbishness should abound; the surprising thing would be if it did not abound. Even with ourselves, who by a seven years' struggle burst the faery dream a century ago, that least erected spirit rears its loathly head from the dust at times, and in our polite press we can read much if we otherwise see nothing of its subtle influence. But no evil is without its compensating good, and the good of English snobbishness is that it has reduced loyalty, whether to the prince or to the patrician, from a political to a social significance. That is, it does so with the upper classes; with the lower, loyalty finds expression in an unparalleled patriotism. An Englishman of the humble or the humbler life may know very well that he is not much in himself; but he believes that England stands for him, and that royalty and nobility stand for England. Both of these, there, are surrounded by an atmosphere of reverence wholly inconceivable to the natives of a country where there are only millionaires to revere.

W. D. Howells

IV

The most curious thing is that the persons in the faery dream seem to believe it as devoutly as the simplest and humblest of the dreamers. The persons in the dream apparently take themselves as seriously as if there were or could be in reality kings and lords. They could not, of course, do so if they were recently dreamed, as they were, say, in the France of the Third Empire. There, one fancies, these figments must have always been smiling in each other's faces when they were by themselves. But the faery dream holds solidly in England because it is such a very old dream. Besides, the dream does not interfere with the realities; it even honors them. If a man does any great thing in England, the chief figure of the faery dream recognizes his deed, stoops to him, lifts him up among the other figures, and makes him part of the dream forever. After that he has standing, such as no man may have with us for more than that psychological moment, when all the papers cry him up, and then everybody tries to forget him. But, better than this, the dream has the effect, if it has not the fact, of securing every man in his place, so long as he keeps to it. Nowhere else in the world is there so much personal independence, without aggression, as in England. There is apparently nothing of it in Germany; in Italy, every one is so courteous and kind that there is no question of it; in the French Republic and in our own, it exists in an excess that is molestive and invasive; in England alone does it strike the observer as being of exactly the just measure.

Very likely the observer is mistaken, and in the present case he will not insist. After all, even the surface indications in such matters are slight and few. But what I noted was that, though the simple and humble have to go to the wall, and for the most part go to it unkicking, in England they were, on their level, respectfully and patiently entreated. At a railroad junction one evening, when there was a great hurrying up stairs and down, and a mad seeking of wrong trains by right people, the company's servants who were taking tickets, and directing passengers this way and that, were patiently kind with futile old men and women, who came up, in the midst of their torment, and pestered them with questions as to the time when trains that had not arrived would leave after they did arrive. I shuddered to think what would have at least verbally happened to such inquirers with us; but, there, not only their lives but their feelings were safe, and they could go away with such self-respect as they had quite intact.

W. D. Howells

V

In no country less good-hearted than England could anything so wrong-headed as the English baggage system be suffered. But, there, passengers of all kinds help the porters to sort their trunks from other people's trunks, on arrival at their stations, and apparently think it no hardship. The porters, who do not seem especially inspired persons, have a sort of guiding instinct in the matter, and wonderfully seldom fail to get the things together for the cab, or to get them off the cab, and, duly labelled, into the luggage-van. Once, at a great junction, my porter seemed to have missed my train, and after vain but not unconsidered appeals to the guard, I had to start without it. At the next station, the company telegraphed back at its own cost the voluminous message of my anxiety and indignation, and I was assured that the next train would bring my valise from Crewe to Edinburgh. When I arrived at Edinburgh, I casually mentioned my trouble to a guard whom I had not seen before. He asked how the bags were marked, and then he said they had come with us. My porter had run with them to my train, but in despair of getting to my car with his burden, had put them into the last luggage-van, and all I had to do was now to identify them at my journey's end.

Why one does not, guiltily or guiltlessly, claim other people's baggage, I do not know; but apparently it is not the custom. Perhaps in this, the deference for any one within his rights, peculiar to the faery dream, operates the security of the respective owners of baggage that could otherwise easily be the general prey. While I saw constant regard paid for personal rights, I saw only one case in which they were offensively asserted. This was in starting from York for London, when we attempted to take possession of a compartment we had paid for from the nearest junction, in order to make certain of it. We found it in the keeping of a gentleman who had turned it from a non-smoking into a smoking compartment, and bestrewn it with his cigar ashes. When told by the porters that we had engaged the compartment, he refused to stir, and said that he had paid for his seat, and he should not leave it till he was provided with another. In vain they besought him to consider our hard case, in being kept out of our own, and promised him another place as good as the one he held. He said that he would not believe it till he saw it, and as he would not go to see it, and it could not be brought to him, there appeared little chance of our getting rid of him. I thought it best to let him and the porters fight it out among themselves. When a force of guards appeared, they were equally ineffective against the intruder, who could not, or did not, say that he did not know the compartment was engaged. Suddenly, for no reason, except that he had sufficiently stood, or sat, upon his rights, he rose, and the others precipitated themselves upon his hand-baggage, mainly composed of fishing- tackle, such as a gentleman carries who has been asked to somebody's fishing, and bore it away to another part of the train. They left one piece behind, and the porter who came back for it was radiantly smiling, as if the struggle had been an agreeable exercise, and he spoke of his antagonist without the least exasperation; evidently, he regarded him as one who had justly defended himself from corporate aggression; his sympathies were with him rather than with us, perhaps because we had not so vigorously asserted ourselves.

W. D. Howells

VI

A case in which a personal wrong rather than a personal right was offensively asserted, was that of a lady, young and too fair to be so unfair, in a crowded train coming from the Doncaster Races to York. She had kept a whole first-class compartment to herself, putting her maid into the second-class adjoining, and heaping the vacant seats with her hand-baggage, which had also overflowed into the corridor. At the time the train started she was comforting herself in her luxurious solitude with a cup of tea, and she stood up, as if to keep other people out. But, after waiting, seven of us, in the corridor, until she should offer to admit us, we all swarmed in upon her, and made ourselves indignantly at home. When it came to that she offered no protest, but gathered up her belongings, and barricaded herself with them. Among the rest there was a typewriting-machine, but what manner of young lady she was, or whether of the journalistic or the theatrical tribe, has never revealed itself to this day. We could not believe that she was very high-born, not nearly so high, for instance, as the old lady who helped dispossess her, and who, when we ventured the hope that it would not rain on the morrow, which was to be St. Leger Day, almost lost the kindness for us inspired by some small service, because we had the bad taste to suggest such a possibility for so sacred a day.

I never saw people standing in a train, except that once which I have already noted, when in a very crowded car in Wales, two women, decent elderly persons, got in and were suffered to remain on foot by the young men who had comfortable places; no one dreamed, apparently, of offering to give up his seat. But, on the other hand, a superior civilization is shown in what I may call the manual forbearance of the trolley and railway folk, who are so apt to nudge and punch you at home here, when they wish your attention. The like happened to me only once in England, and that was at Liverpool, where the tram conductor, who laid hands on me instead of speaking, had perhaps been corrupted by the unseen American influences of a port at which we arrive so abundantly and indiscriminately. I did not resent the touch, though it is what every one is expected to do, if aggrieved, and every one else does it in England. Within his rights, every one is safe; though there may be some who have no rights. If there were, I did not see them, and I suppose that, as an alien, I might have refused to stand up and uncover when the band began playing *God Save the King*, as it did at the end of every musical occasion; I might have urged that, being no subject of the King, I did not feel bound to join in the general prayer. But that would have been churlish, and, where every one had been so civil to me, I did not see why I should not be civil to the King, in a small matter. In the aggregate indeed, it is not a small matter, and I suppose that the stranger always finds the patriotism of a country molestive. Patriotism is, at any rate, very disagreeable, with the sole exception of our own, which we are constantly wishing to share with other people, especially with English people. We spare them none of it, even in their own country, and yet many of us object to theirs; I feel that I am myself being rather offensive about it, now, at this distance from them. Upon the whole, not caring very actively for us, one way or the other, they take it amiably; they try to get our point of view, and, as if it were a thorn, self-sacrificially press their bosoms against it, in the present or recent *entente cordiale*. None of their idiosyncrasies is more notable than their patience, their kindness with our divergence from them; but I am not sure that, having borne with us when we are by, they do not take it out of us when we are away.

We are the poetry of a few, who, we like to think, have studied the most deeply into the causes of our being, or its excuses. But you cannot always be enjoying poetry, and I could well imagine that our lovers must sometimes prefer to shut the page. The common gentleness comes from the common indifference, and from something else that I will not directly touch upon. What is certain is that, with all manner of strangers, the English seem very gentle, when they meet in chance encounter. The average level of good manners is high. My experience was not the widest, and I am always owning it was not deep; but, such as it was, it brought me to the distasteful conviction that in England I did not see the mannerless uncouthness which I often see in America, not so often from high to low, or from old to young, but the reverse. There may be much more than we infer, at the moment, from the modulated voices, which sweetens casual intercourse, but there are certain terms of respect, almost unknown to us, which more obviously do that effect. It is a pity that democracy, being the fine thing it essentially is, should behave so rudely. Must we come to family government, in order to be filial or fraternal in our bearing with one another? Why should we be so blunt, so sharp, so ironical, so brutal in our kindness?

VII

The single-mindedness of the English is beautiful. It may not help to the instant understanding of our jokes; but then, even we are not always joking, and it does help to put us at rest and to make us feel safe. The Englishman may not always tell the truth, but he makes us feel that we are not so sincere as he; perhaps there are many sorts of sincerity. But there is something almost caressing in the kindly pause that precedes his perception of your meaning, and this is very pleasing after the sense of always having your hearer instantly onto you. When, by a chance indefinitely rarer than it is with us at home, one meets an Irishman in England, or better still an Irishwoman, there is an instant lift of the spirit; and, when one passes the Scotch border, there is so much lift that, on returning, one sinks back into the embrace of the English temperament, with a sigh for the comfort of its soft unhurried expectation that there is really something in what you say which, will be clear by-and-by.

Having said so much as this in compliance with the frequent American pretence that the English are without humor, I wish to hedge in the interest of truth. They certainly are not so constantly joking as we; it does not apparently seem to them that fate can be propitiated by a habit of pleasantry, or that this is so merry a world that one need go about grinning in it. Perhaps the conditions with most of them are harder than the conditions with most of us. But, thinking of certain Englishmen I have known, I should be ashamed to join in the cry of those story- telling Americans whose jokes have sometimes fallen effectless. It is true that, wherever the Celt has leavened the doughier Anglo-Saxon lump, the expectation of a humorous sympathy is greater; but there are subtle spirits of Teutonic origin whose fineness we cannot deny, whose delicate gayety is of a sort which may well

W. D. Howells

leave ours impeaching itself of a heavier and grosser fibre.

No doubt you must sometimes, and possibly oftenest, go more than half-way for the response to your humorous intention. Those subtile spirits are shy, and may not offer it an effusive welcome. They are also of such an exquisite honesty that, if they do not think your wit is funny, they will not smile at it, and this may grieve some of our jokers. But, if you have something fine and good in you, you need not be afraid they will fail of it, and they will not be so long about finding it out as some travellers say. When it comes to the grace of the imaginative in your pleasantry, they will be even beforehand with you. But in their extreme of impersonality they will leave the initiative to you in the matter of humor as in others. They will no more seek out your peculiar humor than they will name you in speaking with you.

VIII

Nothing in England seeks you out, except the damp. Your impressions, you have to fight for them. What you see or hear seems of accident. The sort of people you have read of your whole life, and are most intimate with in fiction, you must surprise. They no more court observance than the birds in whose seasonable slaughter society from the King down delights. In fact, it is probable that, if you looked for both, you would find the gunner shyer than the gunned. The pheasant and the fox are bred to give pleasure by their chase; they are tenderly cared for and watched over and kept from harm at the hands of all who do not wish to kill them for the joy of killing, and they are not so elusive but they can be seen by easy chance. The pheasant especially has at times all but the boldness of the barnyard in his fearless port. Once from my passing train, I saw him standing in the middle of a ploughed field, erect, distinct, like a statue of himself, commemorative of the long ages in which his heroic death and martyr sufferance have formed the pride of princes and the peril of poachers. But I never once saw him shot, though almost as many gunners pursue him as there are pheasants in the land. This alone shows how shy the gunners are; and when once I saw the trail of a fox-hunt from the same coign of vantage without seeing the fox, I felt that I had almost indecently come upon the horse and hounds, and that the pink coats and the flowery spread of the dappled dogs over the field were mine by a kind of sneak as base as killing a fox to save my hens.

W. D. Howells

IX

Equally with the foxes and the pheasants, the royalties and nobilities abound in English novels, which really form the chief means of our acquaintance with English life; but the chances that reveal them to the average unintroduced, unpresented American are rarer. By these chances, I heard, out of the whole peerage, but one lord so addressed in public, and that was on a railroad platform where a porter was reassuring him about his luggage. Similarly, I once saw a lady of quality, a tall and girlish she, who stood beside her husband, absently rubbing with her glove the window of her motor, and whom but for the kind interest of our cabman we might never have known for a duchess. It is by their personal uninsistence largely, no doubt, that the monarchy and the aristocracy exist; the figures of the faery dream remain blent with the background, and appear from it only when required to lay cornerstones, or preside at races, or teas or bazars, or to represent the masses at home and abroad, and invisibly hold the viewless reins of government.

Yet it must not be supposed that the commoner sort of dreamers are never jealous of these figments of their fancy. They are often so, and rouse themselves to self-assertion as frequently as our Better Element flings off the yoke of Tammany. At a fair, open to any who would pay, for some forgotten good object, such as is always engaging the energies of society, I saw moving among the paying guests the tall form of a nobleman who had somehow made himself so distasteful to his neighbors that they were not his friends, and regularly voted down his men, whether they stood for Parliament or County Council, and whether they were better than the popular choice or not. As a matter of fact, it was said that they were really better, but the people would not have them because they were his; and one of the theories of

English manliness is that the constant pressure from above has toughened the spirit and enabled Englishmen to stand up stouter and straighter each in his place, just as it is contended elsewhere that the aesthetic qualities of the human race have been heightened by its stresses and deprivations in the struggle of life.

For my own part, I believe neither the one theory nor the other. People are the worse for having people above them, and are the ruder and coarser for having to fight their way. If the triumph of social inequality is such that there are not four men in London who are not snobs, it cannot boast itself greater than the success of economic inequality with ourselves, among whom the fight for money has not produced of late a first-class poet, painter, or sculptor. The English, if they are now the manliest people under the sun, have to thank not their masters but themselves, and a nature originally so generous that no abuse could lastingly wrong it, no political absurdity spoil it. But if this nature had been left free from the beginning, we might see now a nation of Englishmen who, instead of being bound so hard and fast in the bonds of an imperial patriotism, would be the first in a world-wide altruism. Yet their patriotism is so devout that it may well pass itself off upon them for a religious emotion, instead of the superstition which seems to the stranger the implication of an England in the next world as well as in this.

X

We fancy that, because we have here an Episcopal Church, with its hierarchy, we have something equivalent to the English Church. But that is a mistake. The English Church is a part of the whole of English life, as the army or navy is; in English crowds, the national priest is not so frequent as the national soldier, but he is of as marked a quality, and as distinct from the civil world, in uniform, bearing, and aspect; in the cathedral towns, he and his like form a sort of spiritual garrison. At home here you may be ignorant of the feasts of the Episcopal Church without shame or inconvenience; but in England you had better be versed in the incidence of all the holy days if you would stand well with other men, and would know accurately when the changes in the railroad time-tables will take place. It will not do to have ascertained the limits of Lent; you must be up in the Michaelmases and Whitmondays, and the minor saints' days. When once you have mastered this difficult science, you will realize what a colossal transaction the disestablishment of the English Church in England would be, and how it would affect the whole social fabric.

But, even when you have learned your lesson, it will not be to you as that knowledge which has been lived, and which has no more need ever to question itself than the habitual pronunciation of words. If one has moved in good English society, one has no need ever to ask how a word is pronounced, far less to go to the dictionary; one pronounces it as one has always heard it pronounced. The sense of this gives the American a sort of despair, like that of a German or French speaking foreigner, who perceives that he never will be able to speak English. The American is rather worse off, for he has to subdue an inward rebellion, and to form even the wish to pronounce some English words as the English do.

He has, for example, always said "financier," with the accent on the last syllable; and if he has consulted his Webster he has found that there was no choice for him. Then, when he hears it pronounced at Oxford by the head of a college with the accent on the second syllable, and learns on asking that it is never otherwise accented in England, his head whirls a little, and he has a sick moment, in which he thinks he had better let the verb "to be" govern the accusative as the English do, and be done with it, or else telegraph for his passage home at once. Or stop! He must not "telegraph," he must "wire."

W. D. Howells

XI

As for that breathing in the wrong place which is known as dropping one's aitches, I found that in the long time between the first and last of my English sojourns, there had arisen the theory that it was a vice purely cockney in origin, and that it had grown upon the nation through the National Schools. It is grossly believed, or boldly pretended, that till the National School teachers had conformed to the London standard in their pronunciation the wrong breathing was almost unknown in England, but that now it was heard everywhere south of the Scottish border. Worse yet, the teachers in the National Schools had scattered far and wide that peculiar intonation, that droll slip or twist of the vowel sounds by which the cockney alone formerly proclaimed his low breeding, and the infection is now spread as far as popular learning. Like the wrong breathing, it is social death "to any he that utters it," not indeed that swift extinction which follows having your name crossed by royalty from the list of guests at a house where royalty is about to visit, but a slow, insidious malady, which preys upon its victim, and finally destroys him after his life-long struggle to shake it off. It is even worse than the wrong breathing, and is destined to sweep the whole island, where you can nowhere, even now, be quite safe from hearing a woman call herself "a lydy." It may indeed be the contagion of the National School teacher, but I feel quite sure, from long observation of the wrong breathing, that the wrong breathing did not spread from London through the schools, but was everywhere as surely characteristic of the unbred in England as nasality is with us. Both infirmities are of national origin and extent, and both are individual or personal in their manifestation. That is, some Americans in every part of the Union talk through their noses; some Englishmen in every part of the kingdom drop their aitches.

The English-speaking Welsh often drop their aitches, as the English-speaking French do, though the Scotch and Irish never drop them, any more than the Americans, or the English of the second generation among us; but the extremely interesting and great little people of Wales are otherwise as unlike the English as their mother-language is. They seem capable of doing anything but standing six feet in their stockings, which is such a very common achievement with the English, but that is the fault of nature which gave them dark complexions and the English fair. Where the work of the spirit comes in, it effects such a difference between the two peoples as lies between an Eisteddfod and a horse-race. While all the singers of Wales met in artistic emulation at their national musical festival at Rhyl, all the gamblers of England met in the national pastime of playing the horses at Doncaster. More money probably changed hands on the events at Doncaster than at Rhyl, and it was characteristic of the prevalent influence in the common civilization (if there is a civilization common to both races) that the King was at Doncaster and not at Rhyl. But I do not say this to his disadvantage, for I was myself at Doncaster and not at Rhyl. You cannot, unless you have a very practised ear, say which is the finer singer at an Eisteddfod, but almost any one can see which horse comes in first at a race.

W. D. Howells

XII

What is most striking in the mixture of strains in England is that it apparently has not ultimately mixed them; and perhaps after a thousand years the racial traits will be found marking Americans as persistently. We now absorb, and suppose ourselves to be assimilating, the different voluntary and involuntary immigrations; but doubtless after two thousand years the African, the Celt, the Scandinavian, the Teuton, the Gaul, the Hun, the Latin, the Slav will be found atavistically asserting his origin in certain of their common posterity. The Pennsylvania Germans have as stolidly maintained their identity for two centuries as the Welsh in Great Britain for twenty, or, so far as history knows, from the beginning of time. The prejudices of one British stock concerning another are as lively as ever, apparently, however the enmities may have worn themselves away. One need not record any of these English prejudices concerning the Scotch or Irish; they are too well known; but I may set down the opinion of a lively companion in a railroad journey that the Welsh are "the prize liars of the universe." He was an expert accountant by profession, and his affairs took him everywhere in the three Kingdoms, and this was his settled error; for the Welsh themselves know that, if they sometimes seem the prey of a lively imagination, it is the philologically noted fault of their language, which refuses to lend itself to the accurate expression of fact, but which would probably afford them terms for pronouncing the statement of my accountant inexact. He was perhaps a man of convictions rather than conclusions, for, though he was a bright intelligence, of unusually varied interests, there were things that had never appealed to him. We praised together the lovely September landscape through which we were running, and I ventured some remark upon the large holdings of the land: a thing that always saddened me in the face of nature with the reflection that those who tilled the soil owned none of it; though I ought to have remembered the times when the soil owned them, and taken heart. My notion seemed to strike him for the first time, but he dismissed the fact as a necessary part of the English system; it had never occurred to him that there could be question of that system. There must be many Englishmen to whom it does occur, but if you do not happen to meet them you cannot blame the others.

I fancied that one of the Englishmen to whom it might have occurred was he whom I met in Wales at Aberystwyth, where we spoke together a moment in the shadow of the co-educational University there, and who seemed at least of a different mind concerning the Welsh. "These Welsh farmers," he said, "send their sons and daughters to college as if it were quite the natural thing to do. But just imagine a Dorsetshire peasant sending his boy to a University!"

We suppose that the large holdings of land are the effect of wrongs and abuses now wholly in the past, and that the causes for their increase are no longer operative, but are something like those geological laws by which the strata under them formed themselves. Once, however, in driving through the most beautiful part of England, which I will not specify because every part of England is the most beautiful, I came upon an illustration of the reverse, as signal as the spectacle of a landslide. It was the accumulation, not merely within men's memories, but within the actual generation, of vast bodies of land in the hold of a great nobleman who had contrived a title in them by the simple device of enclosing the people's commons. It was a wrong, but there was no one of the wronged who was brave enough or rich enough to dispute it through the broken law, and no witness public-spirited enough to come to their aid. Such things make us think patiently, almost proudly, of our national foible of graft, which may really be of feudal origin. Doubtless the aggression was attacked in the press, but we all know what the attacks of the press amount to against the steadfast will of a powerful corporation, and a great nobleman in England is a powerful corporation. In this instance he had not apparently taken the people's land without some wish to make them a return for it. He had built a handsome road through their property, which he maintained in splendid condition, and he allowed them to drive over his road, and to walk freely in certain portions of their woods. He had also built a magnificent hospital for them, and it seemed rather hard, then, to hear that one of the humblest of them had been known to speak of him in whispered confidence as a "Upas tree."

XIII

Probably he was not personally a Upas tree, probably the rancor toward him left from being bawled after by one of his gatemen at a turning we had taken in his enclosure, "That's a private path!" was unjust. There was no sign, such as everywhere in England renders a place secure from intrusion. The word "Private" painted up anywhere does the effect of bolts and bars and of all obsolete man-traps beyond it, and is not for a moment that challenge to the wayfaring foot which it seems so often with us; but the warnings to the public which we make so mandatory, the English language with unfailing gentleness. You are not told to keep your foot or your wheel to a certain pathway; you are "requested," and sometimes even "kindly requested"; I do not know but once I was "respectfully requested." Perhaps that nobleman's possession of these lands was so new that his retainers had to practise something of unwonted rudeness in keeping it wholly his where he chose. At any rate, the rule of civility is so universal that the politeness from class to class is, for what the stranger sees, all but unfailing. I dare say he does not see everything, even the Argus-eyed American, but apparently the manners of the lower class, where they have been touched by the upper, have been softened and polished to the same consistence and complexion. When it comes to the proffers, and refusals, and insistences, and acceptances between people of condition, such as I witnessed once in a crowded first-class carriage from London on an Oxford holiday, nothing could be more gently urgent, more beautifully forbearing. If the writers of our romantic novels could get just those manners into their fiction, I should not mind their dealing so much with the English nobility and gentry; for those who intend being our nobility and gentry, by-and-by, could not do better than study such high-breeding.

W. D. Howells

If we approach the morals of either superiors or inferiors, we are in a region where it behooves us to tread carefully. To be honest, I know nothing about them, and I will not assume to know anything. I heard from authority which I could not suspect of posing for omniscience that the English rustics were apt to be very depraved, but they may on the other hand be saints for all that I can prove against them. They are superstitious, it is said, and there are few villages or old houses that have not their tutelary spectres. The belief in ghosts is almost universal among the people; as I may allow without superiority, for I do not know but I believe in them myself, and there are some million of American spiritualists who make an open profession of faith in them. It is said also that the poor in England are much spoiled by the constant aid given them in charity. This is supposed to corrupt them, and to make them dependent upon the favors of fortune, rather than the sweat of their brows. On the other hand, they often cannot get work, as I infer from the armies of the unemployed, and, in these cases, I cannot hold them greatly to blame if they bless their givers by their readiness to receive. If one may infer from the incessant beneficences, and the constant demands for more and more charities, one heaped upon another, there are more good objects in England than anywhere else under the sun, for one only gives to good objects, of course. The oppression of the subscriptions is tempered by the smallness of the sum which may satisfy them. "Five shillings is a subscription," said a friend who was accused of really always giving five pounds.

XIV

The English rich do not give so spectacularly as our rich do—that is, by handfuls of millions, but then the whole community gives more, I think, than our community does, and when it does not give, the necessary succor is taxed out of its incomes and legacies. I do not mean that there is no destitution, but only that the better off seem to have the worse off more universally and perpetually in mind than with us. All this is believed to be very demoralizing to the poor, and doubtless the certainty of soup and flannel is bad for the soul of an old woman whose body is doubled up with rheumatism. The Church seems to blame for much of the evil that ensues from giving something to people who have nothing; but I dare say the Dissenters are also guilty.

Just how much is wanted to stay the stomach of a healthy pauper, it would be hard to say; but now and then the wayfarer gets some hint of the frequency if not the amount of feeding among the poor who are able to feed themselves. One day, in the outskirts—they were very tattered and draggled—of Liverpool, we stopped at a pastry-shop, where the kind woman "thought she could accommodate" us with a cup of tea, though she was terribly pressed with custom from all sorts of minute maids and small boys coming in for "penn'orths" of that frightful variety of tart and cake which dismays the beholder from innumerable shop windows in England. When we were brought our safer refection, we noted her activities to the hostess, and she said, "Yes, they all want a bit of cake with their tea, even the poorest"; and when we ventured our supposition that they made their afternoon tea the last meal of the day, she laughed at the notion. "Last meal! They have a good supper before they go to bed. Indeed, they all want their four meals a day."

W. D. Howells

Another time, thriftily running in a third-class carriage from Crewe to Chester, I was joined by a friendly man who addressed me with the frank cordiality of the lower classes in recognizing one of their sort. "They don't know how to charge!" he said, with an irony that referred to the fourpence he had been obliged to pay for a cup of station tea; and when I tried to allege some mitigating facts in behalf of the company, he readily became autobiographical. The transition from tea to eating generally was easy, and he told me that he was a plumber, going to do a job of work at Llandudno, where he had to pay fourteen bob, which I knew to be shillings and mentally translated into $3.50, a week for his board. His wages were $1.50 a day, which the reader who multiplies fourpence by twenty, to make up the difference in money values, will find to be the wages of a good mechanic in the first Edward's time, five hundred years ago. On this he professed to live very well. He rose every morning at half-past four, and at six he had a breakfast of bread, butter, and coffee; at nine he had porridge and coffee; at one, he had soup, meat, and eggs, and perhaps beer; at night, after he got home from work, he had a stew and a bit of meat, and perhaps beer, with Mother. He thought that English people ate too much, generally, and especially on Sunday, when they had nothing else to do. Most men never came home without asking, "Well, Mother, what have you got for me to eat now?" When I remembered how sparely our farm people and mechanics fared, I thought that he was right, or they were wrong; for the puzzling fact remained that they looked gaunt and dyspeptic, and he hale and fresh, though the difference may have had as much to do with the air as the food. I liked him, and I cannot leave him without noting that he was of the lean-faced, slightly aquiline British type, with a light mustache; he was well dressed and well set up, and he spoke strongly, as North Britons do, with nothing of our people's husky whine. I found him on further acquaintance of anti-Chamberlain politics, pro-Boer as to the late war, and rather socialistic. He blamed the labor men for not choosing labor men to office instead of the gentry who offered themselves. He belonged to a plumbers' union, and he had nothing to complain of, but he inferred that the working-man was better off in America, from the fact that none of his friends who had gone to the States ever came home to stay, though they nearly all came home for a holiday, sooner or later. He differed from my other friend, the accountant, in being very fond of the Welsh; it must be owned their race seemed to have acquired merit with him through the tip of two sovereigns which his last employer in Llandudno had given him. On the other hand, he had no love for the Italians who were coming in, especially at Glasgow. In Glasgow, he said, there were more drunken women than anywhere else in the world, though there was no public-house drinking with them as in London. This, so far as I got at it, formed his outlook on life, but I dare say there was more of it.

W. D. Howells

XV

I was always regretting that I got at the people so little, and that only chance hints of what they were thinking and feeling reached me. Now and then, a native observer said something about them which seemed luminous. "We are frightfully feudal," such an observer said, "especially the poor." He did not think it a fault, I believe, and only used his adverb intensifyingly, for he was of a Tory mind. He meant the poor among the country people, who have at last mastered that principle of the feudal system which early enabled the great nobles to pay nothing for the benefits they enjoyed from it. But my other friend, the plumber, was not the least feudal, or not so feudal as many a lowly ward- heeler in New York, who helps to make up the muster of some captain of politics, under the lead of a common boss. The texture of society, in the smarter sense, the narrower sense, is what I could not venture to speak of more confidently. Once I asked a friend, a very dear and valued friend, whether a man's origin or occupation would make any difference in his social acceptance, if he were otherwise interesting and important. He seemed not to know what I would be at, and, when he understood, he responded with almost a shout of amazement, "Oh, not the least in the world!" But I have my doubts still; and I should say that it might be as difficult for a very cultivated and agreeable man servant to get on in London society, as for an artist or poet to feel at home in the first circles of New York. Possibly, however, London society, because of its almost immeasurable vastness, can take in more of more sorts of people, without the consciousness of differences which keeps our own first circles so elect. I venture, somewhat wildly, somewhat unwarrantably, the belief that English society is less sensitive to moral differences than ours, and that people with their little *taches* would find less anxiety in London than in New York lest they should come off on the people they rubbed against. Some Americans, who, even with our increasing prevalence of divorces, are not well seen at home, are cheerfully welcomed in England.

Perhaps, there, all Americans, good and bad, high and low, coarse and fine, are the same to senses not accustomed to our varying textures and shades of color; that is a matter I should be glad to remand to the psychologist, who will have work enough to do if he comes to inquire into such mysteries. One can never be certain just how the English take us, or how much, or whether they take us at all. Oftenest I was inclined to think that we were imperceptible to them, or that, when we were perceptible, they were aware of us as Swedenborg says the most celestial angels are aware of evil spirits, merely as something angular. Americans were distressful to their consciousness, they did not know why; and then they tried to ignore us. But perhaps this is putting it a little fantastically. What I know is that one comes increasingly to reserve the fact of one's nationality, when it is not essential to the occasion, and to become as much as possible an unknown quality, rather than a quality aggressive or positive. Sometimes, when I could feel certain of my ground, I ventured my conviction that Englishmen were not so much interested in Americans as those Americans who stayed at home were apt to think; but when I once expressed this belief to a Unitarian minister, whom I met in the West of England, he received it with surprise and refusal. He said that in his own immediate circle, at least, his friends were interested and increasingly interested in America, what she was and what she meant to be, and still looked toward her for the lead in certain high things which Englishmen have ceased to expect of themselves. My impression is that most of the most forward of the English Sociologists regard America as a back number in those political economics which imply equality as well as liberty in the future. They do not see any difference

W. D. Howells

between our conditions and theirs, as regards the man who works for his living with his hands, except that wages are higher with us, and that physically there is more elbow-room, though mentally and morally there is not. Save a little in my Unitarian minister, and this only conjecturally, I did not encounter that fine spirit which in Old England used to imagine the New World we have not quite turned out to be; but once I met an Englishman who had lived in Canada, and who, gentleman-bred as he was, looked back with fond homesickness to the woods where he had taken up land, and built himself a personable house, chiefly with his own hands. He had lived himself out of touch with his old English life in that new country, and had drawn breath in an opener and livelier air which filled his lungs as the home atmosphere never could again.

XVI

Yet he was standing stiffly up for himself, and strewing his convictions and opinions broadcast as the English all do when pressed by circumstance, while we, with none of their shyness, mostly think our thoughts to ourselves. I suppose we do it because we like better than they to seem of one effect with the rest of our kind. In England one sees a variety of dress in men which one rarely sees at home. They dress there not only in keeping with their work and their play, but in the indulgence of any freak of personal fancy, so that in the street of a provincial town, like Bath, for instance, you will encounter in a short walk a greater range of trousers, leggings, caps, hats, coats, jackets, collars, scarfs, boots and shoes, of tan and black, than you would meet at home in a month of Sundays. The differences do not go to the length of fashions, such as reduce our differences to uniformity, and clothe, say, our legs in knickerbockers till it is found everybody is wearing them, when immediately nobody wears them. Only ladies, of fashions beyond men's, gratify caprices like ours, and even these perhaps not voluntarily. In the obedience they show to the rule that they must never wear the same dinner or ball gown twice, it was said (but who can ever find out the truth of such things?) that they sometimes had sent home from the dressmaker's a number of dresses on liking, and wore them in succession, only to return them, all but one at least, as not liked, the dressmaker having found her account in her work being shown in society.

I do not know just what is to be inferred from a social fact or statement like this, but I may say that the devotion to an ideal of social position is far deeper with the English than with us. Whether we spend more or not, I believe that the English live much nearer their incomes than Americans do. I think that we save more out of our earnings than they out of theirs, and that in this we are more like the Continental peoples, the French or the Italians. They spend vastly more on state than we do, because, for one thing, they have more state to spend on. A man may continue to make money in America, and not change his manner of living till he chooses, and he may never change it. Such a thing could not happen to an Englishwoman as happened to the elderly American house-wife who walked through the magnificent house which her husband had bought to surprise her, and sighed out at last, "Well, now I suppose I shall have to keep a girl!" The girl would have been kept from the beginning of her husband's prosperity, and multiplied, till the house was full of servants. If you have the means of a gentleman in England, you must live like a gentleman, apparently; you cannot live plainly, and put by, and largely you must trust to your life-insurance as the fortune you will leave your heirs. It cannot be denied that the more generous expenditure of the English adds to the grace of life, and that they are more hospitable according to their means than we are; or than those Continental peoples who are not hospitable at all.

A thing that one feels more and more irritatingly in England is that, while with other foreigners we stand on common ground, where we may be as unlike them as we choose, with the English we always stand on English ground, where we can differ only at our peril, and to our disadvantage. A person speaking English and bearing an English name, had better be English, for if he cannot it shows, it proves, that there is something wrong in him. Our misfortune is that our tradition, and perhaps our inclination, obliges us to be un-English, whereas we do not trouble ourselves to be un-French, or un-Italian, for we are so by nature. The effort involved in distinguishing ourselves breeds a sort of annoy-ance, or call it no more than uneasiness, which is almost as bad as a bad conscience; and in our sense of hopeless perdition we turn vindictively upon our judge. But that is not fair and it is not wise; he does not mean to be our judge, except when he comes to us for the purpose; in his own house, he is civilly unaware of putting us to any test whatever. If you ask him whether he likes this thing or that of ours, he will tell you frankly; he never can see why he should not be frank; he has a kind of helplessness in always speaking the truth; and he does not try to make it palatable.

W. D. Howells

XVII

An English Radical, who would say of his King no more than that he was a good little man, and most useful in promoting friendship with France, was inclined to blame us because we did not stay by at the time of our Revolution, and help them fight out as Englishmen the fight for English freedom. He had none of the loyalty of sentiment which so mystifies the American, but plenty of the loyalty of reason, and expected a Utopia which should not be of political but of economical cast. But one was always coming upon illustrations of the loyalty of sentiment with which of course one could have no quarrel, for their patriotism seldom concerned us, except rather handsomely to include us. The French have ceased to be the hereditary enemy, and the Russians have now taken their place in the popular patriotism. I always talked with the lower classes when I could, perhaps because I felt myself near them in my unworthy way, and one evening in a grassy lane I made the acquaintance of a friendly man letting his horse browse the wayside turf. He was in the livery-stable line, but he had been a soldier many years. Upon this episode he became freely autobiographical, especially concerning his service in India. He volunteered the declaration that he had had enough of war, but he added, thoughtfully, "I should like to go out for a couple of years if there was any trouble with Russia."

The love of England comes out charmingly in the swarming of English tourists in every part of their country. Americans may sometimes outnumber them at the Continental shrines, but we are in a pitiful minority at the memorable places in England; in fact, we are nowhere beside the natives. I liked their fondness for their own so much that I never could feel the fine scorn for "trippers" which I believe all persons of condition ought to assume. Even when the trippers did not seem very intelligently interested in what they saw, they were harmlessly employed, for a scene of beauty, or of historic appeal, could not be desecrated by the courtships which are constantly going on all over England, especially at the holiday seasons.

The English are, indeed, great holiday-makers, even when past the age of putting their arms around one another's waists. The many and many seaside resorts form the place of their favorite outings, where they try to spend such days and weeks of the late summer as their savings will pay for. It is said that families in very humble station save the year round for these vacations, and, having put by twelve or fifteen pounds, repair to some such waterside as Blackpool, or its analogue in their neighborhood, and lavish them upon the brief joy of the time. They take the cheaper lodgings, and bring with them the less perishable provisions, and lead a life of resolute gayety on the sands and in the sea, and at the pier-ends where the negro minstrels and the Pierrots, who equally abound, make the afternoons and evenings a delight which no one would suspect from their faces to be the wild thing it is. If they go home at the end "high sorrowful and cloyed," there is no forecast of it in their demeanor, which is as little troubled as it is animated. The young people are even openly gay, and the robustness of their flirtations adds sensibly to the interest of the spectator. Our own public lovers seem of a humbler sort, and they mostly content themselves with the passive embraces of which every seat in our parks affords an example; but in England such lovers add playful struggles. A favorite pastime seemed to be for one of them to hold something in the hand, and for the other to try prying it open. When it was the young man who kept his hand shut, the struggle could go on almost indefinitely. I suppose it led to many engagements and marriages.

When the young people were not walking up and down, or

W. D. Howells

playfully scuffling, they were reading novels; in fact, I do not imagine that anywhere else in the world is there a half, or a tenth part, so much fiction consumed as in the English summer resorts. It is probably of the innutritious lightness of pop-corn; I had never the courage to look at the volumes which I could so easily have overlooked; but I am sure it was all out of the circulating library. As there were often several young women to one man, most of the girls had to content themselves with the flirtations in the books, where, I dare say, the heroines were always prying the heroes' hands open. On every seat one found them poring upon the glowing page, and met them in every walk with a volume under the arm, and another clasped to the heart. At places where the hand played, and they were ostensibly listening to the music, they were bowed upon their books, and the flutter of the turning leaves almost silenced the blare of the horns. By what inspiration they knew when *God Save the King* was coming, and rose with a long sigh heaved in common, I should not be able to say. Perhaps they always reached the end of a story at the time the band came to that closing number, or perhaps they felt its imminence in their nerves. The fiction was not confined to the young girls, however. Both sexes and all ages partook of it; I saw as many old girls as young girls reading novels, and mothers of families were apparently as much addicted to the indulgence. I suppose they put by their books when they took tea, which is the other most noticeable dissipation in England. But I cannot enter upon that chapter; it is too large a theme; I will say, merely, that as the saloons are on Sixth Avenue, so the tea- rooms are in every part of the island.

XVIII

It had seemed to me in former visits to England that the Christian Sabbath was a more depressing day there than here, but from the last I have a more cheerful memory of it. I still felt it dispiriting in London, where as many fled from it as could, and where the empty streets symbolized a world abandoned to destruction; but this was mainly in the forenoon. Even then, the markets and fairs in the avenues given up to them were the scenes of an activity which was not without gayety, and certainly not without noise; and when the afternoon came, the lower classes, such as had remained in town, thronged to the public houses, and the upper classes to the evening parade in the Park. As to the relative amount of church-going, I will not even assume to be sure; but I have a fancy that it is a rite much less rigorous than it used to be. Still, in provincial places, I found the churches full on a Sunday morning, and all who could afford it hallowed the day by putting on a frock-coat and a top-hat, which are not worn outside of London on week-days. The women, of course, were always in their best on Sunday. Perhaps in the very country the upper classes go to church as much as formerly, but I have my doubts whether they feel so much obliged to it in conformity to usage, or for the sake of example to their inferiors. Where there are abbeys and minsters and cathedrals, as there are pretty well everywhere in England, religion is an attractive spectacle, and one could imagine people resorting to its functions for aesthetic reasons.

But, in these guesses, one must remember that the English who remained at home were never Puritanized, never in such measure personally conscienced, as those who came to America in the times of the successive Protestant fervors; and that is a thing which we are apt to forget. The

W. D. Howells

home-keeping English continued, with changes of ritual, much like the peoples who still acknowledged as their head "the Bishop of Rome." Their greater morality, if it was greater, was temperamental rather than spiritual, and, leaving the church to look after religion much more than our Puritans did, they kept a simplicity of nature impossible to the sectaries always taking stock of their souls. In fact, the Calvinists of New England were almost essentially different from the Calvinists of Holland, of France, even of Scotland. If our ancestors were the children of light, as they trusted, they were darkened by the forest, into which they plunged, to certain reasons which the children of darkness, as the Puritans believed the non-Puritans to be, saw by the uncertain glimmers from the world about them. There is no denying that with certain great gains, the American Puritans became, in a worldly sense, provincialized, and that if they lived in the spirit, they lived in it narrowly, while the others, who lived in the body, lived in it liberally, or at any rate handsomely. From our narrowness we flattered ourselves that we were able to imagine a life more broadly based than theirs, or at least a life from which theirs must look insufficient and unfinal, so long as man feels within himself the prompting to be something better or higher than he is. Yet the English life is wonderfully perfected. With a faery dream of a king supported in his preeminence by a nobility, a nobility supported in turn by a commonalty, a commonalty supported again by a proletariat resting upon immeasurable ether; with a system of government kept, by assent so general that the dissent does not matter, in the hands of a few families reared, if not trained, to power; with a society so intimately and thoroughly self-acquainted that one touch of gossip makes its whole world kin, and responsive to a single emotion; with a charity so wisely studied, and so carefully applied, that restive misery never quite grows rebellious; with a patriotism so inborn and ingrained that all things English seem righteous because English; with a willingness to share the general well-being quite to the verge, but never beyond the verge, of public control of the administration—with all this, the thing must strike the unbelieving observer as desperately perfect. "They have got it down cold," he must say to himself, and confirm himself in his unfaith by reflecting that it is very cold.

XIX

The best observer of England that ever was, he whose book about the English makes all other comment seem idle and superfluous palaver, that Ralph Waldo Emerson whom we always find ahead of us when we look back for him, was once, as he relates in a closing chapter of English Traits, brought to bay by certain great English friends of his, who challenged him to say whether there really were any Americans with an American idea, and a theory of our future. "Thus challenged, I bethought myself neither of Congress, neither of President nor of Cabinet Ministers, nor of such as would make of America another Europe.... I opened the dogma of no-government and non-resistance, and anticipated the objections and the fun, and procured a kind of hearing for it. I said, It is true that I have never yet seen in any country a man of sufficient valor to stand for this truth, and yet ... 'tis certain, as God liveth, the gun that does not need another gun, the law of love and justice alone, can effect a clean revolution.... I insisted ... that the manifest absurdity of the view to English feasibility could make no difference to a gentleman; that as to our secure tenure of our mutton-chop and spinach in London or in Boston, the soul might quote Talleyrand, '*Messieurs, je n'en vois pas la necessite.*'" In other words, Emerson laid before his great English friends a programme, as nearly as might then be, of philosophical anarchism, and naturally it met with no more acceptance than it would if now presented to the most respectable of his American readers. Yet it is never to be forgotten that it was the English who, with all their weight of feudal tradition, and amidst the nightmares to which their faery dream seemed so long subject, invented the only form of Democratic Christianity the world has yet known, unless indeed the German Mennonites are the same as the earlier English Quakers were in creed and life. In the pseudo-republic of the Cromwellian commonwealth the English had a state as wholly without liberty, equality, and fraternity as in the king-capped oligarchy they had before and have had ever since. We may be sure that they will never have such another commonwealth, or any resembling ours, which can no longer offer itself as an eminent example.

The sort of Englishmen, of whose respect Americans can make surest are those English thick-and-thin patriots who admire force and strength, and believe that it is the Anglo-Saxon mission to possess the earth, and to profit by its weaker peoples, not cruelly, not unkindly, yet unquestionably. The Englishmen of whose disrespect we can make surest are those who expect to achieve liberty, equality, and fraternity in the economic way, the political way having failed; who do not care whether the head of the state is born or elected, is called "King" or called "President," since he will presently not be at all; who abhor war, and believe that the meek shall inherit the earth, and these only if they work for a living. They have already had their will with the existing English state, until now that state is far more the servant of the people in fetching and carrying, in guarding them from hard masters and succoring them in their need, than the republic which professes to derive its just powers from the consent of the governed. When one encounters this sort of Englishman, one thinks silently of the child labor in the South, of the monopolies in the North, of the companies which govern while they serve us, and one hopes that the Englishman is not silently thinking of them too. He is probably of the lower classes, and one consoles one's self as one can by holding one's head higher in better company, where, without secret self-contempt, one can be more openly proud of our increasing fortunes and our increasing territory, and our warlike adequacy to a first position among the nations of the world. There is no fear that in such company one's national susceptibilities will be wounded, or that one

W. D. Howells

will not be almost as much admired for one's money as at home. I do not say quite, because there are still things in England even more admired than money. Certainly a very rich American would be considered in such English society, but certainly he would not be so much considered as an equally rich Englishman who was also a duke.

I cannot name a nobleman of less rank, because I will not belittle my rich countryman, but perhaps the English would think differently, and would look upon him as lower than the latest peer or the newest knight of the King's creation. The King, who has no power, can do almost anything in England; and his touch, which is no longer sovereign for scrofula, can add dignity and give absolute standing to a man whose achievements merit it, but who with us would fail of anything like it. The English system is more logical than ours, but not so reasonable. The English have seen from the beginning inequality and the rule of the few. We can hardly prove that we see, in the future, equality and the rule of the many. Yet our vision is doubtless prophetic, whatever obliquities our frequent astigmatism may impart to it. Meantime, in its ampler range there is room for the play of any misgiving short of denial; but the English cannot doubt the justice of what they have seen without forming an eccentric relation to the actual fact. The Englishman who refuses the formal recognition of his distinction by his prince is the anomaly, not the Englishman who accepts it. Gladstone who declines a peerage is anomalous, not Tennyson who takes it. As part of the English system, as a true believer in the oligarchically administered monarchy, Gladstone was illogical, and Tennyson was logical.

ABOUT THE AUTHOR

 **William Dean Howells** (March 1, 1837 – May 11, 1920) was an American realist author and literary critic.

Born in Martins Ferry, Ohio, originally Martinsville, to William Cooper and Mary Dean Howells, Howells was the second of eight children. His father was a newspaper editor and printer, and the father moved frequently around Ohio. Howells began to help his father with typesetting and printing work at an early age. In 1852, his father arranged to have one of Howells' poems published in the Ohio State Journal without telling him.

He wrote his first novel, The Wedding Journey, in 1872, but his literary reputation took off with the realist novel, A Modern Instance, published in 1882, which described the decay of a marriage. His 1885 novel The Rise of Silas Lapham is perhaps his best known, describing the rise and fall of an American entrepreneur in the paint business. His social views were also strongly reflected in the novels Annie Kilburn (1888) and A Hazard of New Fortunes (1890). He was particularly outraged by the trials resulting from the Haymarket Riot.

In 1904, he was one of the first seven chosen for membership in the American Academy of Arts and Letters, of which he became president.

Choose from Thousands of 1stWorldLibrary Classics By

A. M. Barnard
Ada Leverson
Adolphus William Ward
Aesop
Agatha Christie
Alexander Aaronsohn
Alexander Kielland
Alexandre Dumas
Alfred Gatty
Alfred Ollivant
Alice Duer Miller
Alice Turner Curtis
Alice Dunbar
Allen Chapman
Alleyne Ireland
Ambrose Bierce
Amelia E. Barr
Amory H. Bradford
Andrew Lang
Andrew McFarland Davis
Andy Adams
Angela Brazil
Anna Alice Chapin
Anna Sewell
Annie Besant
Annie Hamilton Donnell
Annie Payson Call
Annie Roe Carr
Annonaymous
Anton Chekhov
Archibald Lee Fletcher
Arnold Bennett
Arthur C. Benson
Arthur Conan Doyle
Arthur M. Winfield
Arthur Ransome
Arthur Schnitzler
Arthur Train
Atticus
B.H. Baden-Powell
B. M. Bower
B. C. Chatterjee
Baroness Emmuska Orczy
Baroness Orczy
Basil King
Bayard Taylor
Ben Macomber
Bertha Muzzy Bower
Bjornstjerne Bjornson

Booth Tarkington
Boyd Cable
Bram Stoker
C. Collodi
C. E. Orr
C. M. Ingleby
Carolyn Wells
Catherine Parr Traill
Charles A. Eastman
Charles Amory Beach
Charles Dickens
Charles Dudley Warner
Charles Farrar Browne
Charles Ives
Charles Kingsley
Charles Klein
Charles Hanson Towne
Charles Lathrop Pack
Charles Romyn Dake
Charles Whibley
Charles Willing Beale
Charlotte M. Braeme
Charlotte M. Yonge
Charlotte Perkins Stetson
Clair W. Hayes
Clarence Day Jr.
Clarence E. Mulford
Clemence Housman
Confucius
Coningsby Dawson
Cornelis DeWitt Wilcox
Cyril Burleigh
D. H. Lawrence
Daniel Defoe
David Garnett
Dinah Craik
Don Carlos Janes
Donald Keyhoe
Dorothy Kilner
Dougan Clark
Douglas Fairbanks
E. Nesbit
E. P. Roe
E. Phillips Oppenheim
E. S. Brooks
Earl Barnes
Edgar Rice Burroughs
Edith Van Dyne
Edith Wharton

Edward Everett Hale
Edward J. O'Biren
Edward S. Ellis
Edwin L. Arnold
Eleanor Atkins
Eleanor Hallowell Abbott
Eliot Gregory
Elizabeth Gaskell
Elizabeth McCracken
Elizabeth Von Arnim
Ellem Key
Emerson Hough
Emilie F. Carlen
Emily Bronte
Emily Dickinson
Enid Bagnold
Enilor Macartney Lane
Erasmus W. Jones
Ernie Howard Pie
Ethel May Dell
Ethel Turner
Ethel Watts Mumford
Eugene Sue
Eugenie Foa
Eugene Wood
Eustace Hale Ball
Evelyn Everett-green
Everard Cotes
F. H. Cheley
F. J. Cross
F. Marion Crawford
Fannie E. Newberry
Federick Austin Ogg
Ferdinand Ossendowski
Fergus Hume
Florence A. Kilpatrick
Fremont B. Deering
Francis Bacon
Francis Darwin
Frances Hodgson Burnett
Frances Parkinson Keyes
Frank Gee Patchin
Frank Harris
Frank Jewett Mather
Frank L. Packard
Frank V. Webster
Frederic Stewart Isham
Frederick Trevor Hill
Frederick Winslow Taylor

Friedrich Kerst
Friedrich Nietzsche
Fyodor Dostoyevsky
G.A. Henty
G.K. Chesterton
Gabrielle E. Jackson
Garrett P. Serviss
Gaston Leroux
George A. Warren
George Ade
Geroge Bernard Shaw
George Cary Eggleston
George Durston
George Ebers
George Eliot
George Gissing
George MacDonald
George Meredith
George Orwell
George Sylvester Viereck
George Tucker
George W. Cable
George Wharton James
Gertrude Atherton
Gordon Casserly
Grace E. King
Grace Gallatin
Grace Greenwood
Grant Allen
Guillermo A. Sherwell
Gulielma Zollinger
Gustav Flaubert
H. A. Cody
H. B. Irving
H.C. Bailey
H. G. Wells
H. H. Munro
H. Irving Hancock
H. R. Naylor
H. Rider Haggard
H. W. C. Davis
Haldeman Julius
Hall Caine
Hamilton Wright Mabie
Hans Christian Andersen
Harold Avery
Harold McGrath
Harriet Beecher Stowe
Harry Castlemon
Harry Coghill
Harry Houidini

Hayden Carruth
Helent Hunt Jackson
Helen Nicolay
Hendrik Conscience
Hendy David Thoreau
Henri Barbusse
Henrik Ibsen
Henry Adams
Henry Ford
Henry Frost
Henry James
Henry Jones Ford
Henry Seton Merriman
Henry W Longfellow
Herbert A. Giles
Herbert Carter
Herbert N. Casson
Herman Hesse
Hildegard G. Frey
Homer
Honore De Balzac
Horace B. Day
Horace Walpole
Horatio Alger Jr.
Howard Pyle
Howard R. Garis
Hugh Lofting
Hugh Walpole
Humphry Ward
Ian Maclaren
Inez Haynes Gillmore
Irving Bacheller
Isabel Cecilia Williams
Isabel Hornibrook
Israel Abrahams
Ivan Turgenev
J.G.Austin
J. Henri Fabre
J. M. Barrie
J. M. Walsh
J. Macdonald Oxley
J. R. Miller
J. S. Fletcher
J. S. Knowles
J. Storer Clouston
J. W. Duffield
Jack London
Jacob Abbott
James Allen
James Andrews
James Baldwin

James Branch Cabell
James DeMille
James Joyce
James Lane Allen
James Lane Allen
James Oliver Curwood
James Oppenheim
James Otis
James R. Driscoll
Jane Abbott
Jane Austen
Jane L. Stewart
Janet Aldridge
Jens Peter Jacobsen
Jerome K. Jerome
Jessie Graham Flower
John Buchan
John Burroughs
John Cournos
John F. Kennedy
John Gay
John Glasworthy
John Habberton
John Joy Bell
John Kendrick Bangs
John Milton
John Philip Sousa
John Taintor Foote
Jonas Lauritz Idemil Lie
Jonathan Swift
Joseph A. Altsheler
Joseph Carey
Joseph Conrad
Joseph E. Badger Jr
Joseph Hergesheimer
Joseph Jacobs
Jules Vernes
Julian Hawthrone
Julie A Lippmann
Justin Huntly McCarthy
Kakuzo Okakura
Karle Wilson Baker
Kate Chopin
Kenneth Grahame
Kenneth McGaffey
Kate Langley Bosher
Kate Langley Bosher
Katherine Cecil Thurston
Katherine Stokes
L. A. Abbot
L. T. Meade

L. Frank Baum
Latta Griswold
Laura Dent Crane
Laura Lee Hope
Laurence Housman
Lawrence Beasley
Leo Tolstoy
Leonid Andreyev
Lewis Carroll
Lewis Sperry Chafer
Lilian Bell
Lloyd Osbourne
Louis Hughes
Louis Joseph Vance
Louis Tracy
Louisa May Alcott
Lucy Fitch Perkins
Lucy Maud Montgomery
Luther Benson
Lydia Miller Middleton
Lyndon Orr
M. Corvus
M. H. Adams
Margaret E. Sangster
Margret Howth
Margaret Vandercook
Margaret W. Hungerford
Margret Penrose
Maria Edgeworth
Maria Thompson Daviess
Mariano Azuela
Marion Polk Angellotti
Mark Overton
Mark Twain
Mary Austin
Mary Catherine Crowley
Mary Cole
Mary Hastings Bradley
Mary Roberts Rinehart
Mary Rowlandson
M. Wollstonecraft Shelley
Maud Lindsay
Max Beerbohm
Myra Kelly
Nathaniel Hawthrone
Nicolo Machiavelli
O. F. Walton
Oscar Wilde

Owen Johnson
P.G. Wodehouse
Paul and Mabel Thorne
Paul G. Tomlinson
Paul Severing
Percy Brebner
Percy Keese Fitzhugh
Peter B. Kyne
Plato
Quincy Allen
R. Derby Holmes
R. L. Stevenson
R. S. Ball
Rabindranath Tagore
Rahul Alvares
Ralph Bonehill
Ralph Henry Barbour
Ralph Victor
Ralph Waldo Emmerson
Rene Descartes
Ray Cummings
Rex Beach
Rex E. Beach
Richard Harding Davis
Richard Jefferies
Richard Le Gallienne
Robert Barr
Robert Frost
Robert Gordon Anderson
Robert L. Drake
Robert Lansing
Robert Lynd
Robert Michael Ballantyne
Robert W. Chambers
Rosa Nouchette Carey
Rudyard Kipling
Saint Augustine
Samuel B. Allison
Samuel Hopkins Adams
Sarah Bernhardt
Sarah C. Hallowell
Selma Lagerlof
Sherwood Anderson
Sigmund Freud
Standish O'Grady
Stanley Weyman
Stella Benson
Stella M. Francis

Stephen Crane
Stewart Edward White
Stijn Streuvels
Swami Abhedananda
Swami Parmananda
T. S. Ackland
T. S. Arthur
The Princess Der Ling
Thomas A. Janvier
Thomas A Kempis
Thomas Anderton
Thomas Bailey Aldrich
Thomas Bulfinch
Thomas De Quincey
Thomas Dixon
Thomas H. Huxley
Thomas Hardy
Thomas More
Thornton W. Burgess
U. S. Grant
Upton Sinclair
Valentine Williams
Various Authors
Vaughan Kester
Victor Appleton
Victor G. Durham
Victoria Cross
Virginia Woolf
Wadsworth Camp
Walter Camp
Walter Scott
Washington Irving
Wilbur Lawton
Wilkie Collins
Willa Cather
Willard F. Baker
William Dean Howells
William le Queux
W. Makepeace Thackeray
William W. Walter
William Shakespeare
Winston Churchill
Yei Theodora Ozaki
Yogi Ramacharaka
Young E. Allison
Zane Grey

www.ingramcontent.com/pod-product-compliance
Lightning Source LLC
Chambersburg PA
CBHW031335170626
46807CB00002B/708